P9-DGH-760

Wicker, Cane, and Willow

Wicker, Cane, and Willow

Decorating ideas...Step-by-step projects...
Design techniques

BETH FRANKS

Grove Weidenfeld
New York

A FRIEDMAN GROUP BOOK

Copyright © 1990 by Michael Friedman Publishing Group, Inc.

All rights reserved. No part of this publication may be reproduced, stored in a retrieval system, or transmitted, in any form or by any means, electronic, mechanical, photocopying, recording, or otherwise, without the prior written permission of the publisher.

Published in the United States by
Grove Weidenfeld
A Division of Wheatland Corporation
841 Broadway
New York, New York 10003-4793

Library of Congress Cataloging-in-Publication Data

Franks, Beth.
     Wicker, cane, and willow : decorating ideas, step-by-step
projects, design techniques / Beth Franks. — 1st ed.
        p.   cm.
    Bibliography: p.
    ISBN 0-8021-1239-0 (alk. paper)
    1. Wicker furniture.   2. Rattan furniture.   3. Furniture design.
4. Interior decoration.   I. Title.
NK2712.7.F73   1990
749—dc20
                                    89-16457
                                    CIP

WICKER, CANE, AND WILLOW: Decorating ideas . . . Step-by-step projects . . . Design techniques
was prepared and produced by
Michael Friedman Publishing Group
15 West 26th Street
New York, New York 10010

Editor: Sharon Kalman
Art Director: Robert Kosturko
Designer: Devorah Levinrad
Photography Editor: Christopher Bain
Photo Researcher: Daniella Nilva

Typeset by B.P.E. Graphics
Color separations by Kwong Ming Graphicprint
Printed and bound in Singapore by Tien Wah Press (Pte) Ltd

First Edition 1990

10 9 8 7 6 5 4 3 2 1

Dedication

To Mike, with love.

Acknowledgments

I'd like to thank all the crafters, dealers, and manufacturers who responded to my questionnaire and indicated a willingness to be interviewed. Especially Anthony De Francesco at H.H. Perkins, Jo Holland at Conrad Imports, Anthony C. Melkun at Bielecky Brothers, and the folks at Ficks Reed here in Cincinnati. A special thanks to my editor, Sharon Kalman, whose excellent suggestions and meticulous attention to detail helped make this a better book. An extra special thanks goes to Richard Kollath for his crucial help in the creation of the step-by-step projects. And finally, I'd like to thank my parents, who took me to Camp Akita as a child (where I first learned to love Adirondack furniture), and also to my old friend Aliceanne, whose childhood room was filled with whimsical wicker, and who has wicker furniture in her house to this day.

Table of Contents

© Jim Widess

© James R. Levin/FPG International

INTO THE TWENTY-FIRST
CENTURY WITH WICKER,
CANE, AND WILLOW

It has been said that the first human seat was probably a tree branch, and from that humble beginning sprang everything from Chippendale side chairs to modular sofas.

But while we may not know who invented the first chair, we do know that wickerwork is an ancient craft. Woven rush chests have been found in Egyptian tombs dating back to 2000 B.C.; the legendary bulrush basket that sheltered baby Moses may have been a prototype of the wicker bassinets we use today. Stone carvings from the Sumerian and Roman cultures show dignitaries seated on wicker chairs, and woven basket chairs were all the rage in Medieval Europe. Wicker came to America on the *Mayflower*, in the form of a cradle for Peregrine White, who was born during the voyage.

Although it has been used almost continuously throughout history, wicker has gone in and out of style. Its most recent heyday was from 1865 to 1930, when it was very much in vogue as porch and garden furniture; after 1900 it made its way indoors as well. But fashions changed, and suddenly wicker was considered quite gauche, so all the beautiful old pieces were subsequently banished to the attic or city dump.

Then in the 1960s, wicker again began appearing in homes, and it has been gaining popularity ever since. Now, in the final decade of the twentieth century, we're experiencing a renaissance of revivals, and wicker is definitely back in vogue. Because our homes reflect our personalities and our own individual sense of style, modern design is nothing if not eclectic. People now surround themselves with the colors, shapes, and textures that make them happiest, whether these things are all of the same period or not. No longer stereotyped as porch furniture, wicker now makes a valuable contribution to the living room, bathroom, bedroom, dining room, den, office, and family room.

As natural materials, wicker, cane, and willow have the ability to both complement and add a new dimension to any decor. Wicker is very versatile. It can be twisted and turned into almost any shape—from chaises and rockers to lamp shades and floor coverings—in styles ranging from rustic to ornate, with lots of possibilities in between. But before exploring the variety of available options, let's find out exactly what is meant when talking about wicker, cane, and willow.

Right: *Most wicker furniture is made by hand: the crafter weaves coarse fibers around a sturdy frame. An ancient craft, wickerwork arose from the basket-making tradition.*

Since its invention sometime in the 1700s, the rocker has been at home on porches, acting as an unspoken invitation to "sit a spell." President Kennedy used a cane rocker like this one (right) in the White House, and found it soothed his back pain.

© Lynn Karlin

Wicker, cane, and willow are slender, supple branches plaited or woven to make furniture, baskets, and other useful objects.

Wickerwork is created by weaving coarse fibers around a frame that forms the core of the piece. Throughout history, people in different parts of the world have woven furniture out of whatever materials they found at hand. So, while rattan is the chief source for wicker,

objects can also be woven from reed, raffia, fiber rush, buri, various dried grasses, and of course, cane and willow. The following definitions offer a brief introduction to the most commonly used materials and styles.

By strict definition, wicker means "small, pliant twig." It is derived from the Swedish words *wika*, "to bend," and *vikker*, "willow." Practically speaking, however, wicker refers not to the material itself, but to a construction technique.

Courtesy Connecticut Cane & Reed Co.

WICKER MATERIAL AND STYLE GLOSSARY

BAMBOO

A member of the grass family, bamboo sometimes grows to a height of 100 feet (30 meters). Like rattan, bamboo has a tough outer coat that can be stripped off to make cane. It also resembles rattan in that its stalks are used in furniture construction, sometimes as framing for wickerwork. But because bamboo is hollow, it isn't as strong as rattan (which is solid); also, the joints of the bamboo stalk are susceptible to moisture and should be sealed.

BAR HARBOR

A style of wicker featuring an extremely loose weave, so that there are large openings between the latticework. Manufacturers developed the Bar Harbor style in the early 1900s to offset the high cost of labor, since all the work was done by hand; compare with Cape Cod style.

BURI

A very fine, white fiber obtained from the stalks of the unopened leaves of the talipot palm, found in the Philippines.

CANE

Any of various tall, woody reeds with a hollow or pithy, usually slender and flexible, jointed stem (e.g., rattan and some bamboos). Cane also refers to the split surface of rattan or bamboo when it's been cut into very thin strips for weaving chair seats and baskets.

CAPE COD

With the advent of Bar Harbor wicker, the original, closely woven wicker came to be known as Cape Cod style. Although it was more expensive, the public preferred Cape Cod; eventually, with the advent of fiber rush and the Lloyd loom (see fiber rush, below), the public's taste for inexpensive, closely woven wicker was satisfied.

FIBER RUSH

A synthetic material made of twisted paper, used like reed in weaving wicker. Invented in 1904, fiber rush caused a revolution in 1917 when Marshall Lloyd created a loom that would weave large sheets of it, eliminating the laborious handweaving process. Suddenly Cape Cod-style wicker was affordable; but at the same time, it lost some of its unique handmade charm. (More on the pros and cons of fiber rush in Chapter Two.)

RAFFIA

The coarse stalks of the raffia palm, native to Madagascar; dried, they are sometimes used to wrap furniture.

RATTAN

Several hundred species of rattan flourish in India, Southeast Asia, China, and Indonesia; all have long fibrous stalks covered with tough bark. Technically a palm, rattan grows more like a vine: its leaves have long, barbed tips that allow it to cling to other trees, reaching heights of 500 to

600 feet (152 to 183 meters), though only 1½ inches (4 centimeters) in diameter.

To process rattan, the bark is removed and cut into long, thin strips for cane seats and chair backs; the pithy interior is then cut into reed for wickerwork. Sometimes the entire "pole" is used to make furniture—it looks like bamboo but is much stronger. Rattan is strong enough to be its own frame and can be fastened as securely as wood; when steamed, it will bend into a variety of shapes without cracking.

REED

Cut from the pithy interior of the rattan stalk, reed is available in various sizes and shapes: round, flat, and half round. Reed is what's most often used to weave wicker; it can be left natural or painted. (Reed is also the name for several plants in the grass family that are dried and used to make such things as baskets and reed pipes.)

RUSH

Common, or bog, rush grows wild in swamps, along riverbanks, and in moist places all over the northern hemisphere. (The species most often used to make rush seats is familiar to most of us as the cattail.) Dried rush is soaked in water, then woven piece by piece into a rope of rush; hence, the resemblance to twine. One rope is then interwoven with another, directly on the frame, to create a rush seat. Rush is sometimes used to make baskets and floor mats, but because it's complicated and time-consuming to work with, nowadays fiber rush is often substituted for natural rush.

SEA GRASS

Also called Oriental or China sea grass, the dried stems of this tassel grass are hand-twisted to look like rope, then used to weave baskets or wicker furniture.

© Stanley Joseph

SISAL

This widely cultivated West Indian agave yields a durable white fiber that's used for twine and floor mats, among other things.

WILLOW

Willow trees grow worldwide; there are one hundred different species in the United States alone. Branches (or osiers) from willow trees are stripped of their leaves, then dried; later, these osiers are made into wicker furniture or baskets. Rustic bent willow furniture is distinguished from wicker in that it isn't woven, but constructed from benders—taller, sturdier trees used for sofas, etc., and from whips—slimmer trees used for chair arms and backs, etc.

Willow osiers, stripped of their leaves, are sorted by size and gathered into bunches (left).

© Steven Brooke

Chapter One

WICKER, CANE, AND WILLOW THROUGHOUT THE HOME

Wickerwork, bent willow, and caned or rush-bottomed furniture add texture and personality to just about any decorating scheme, in any room of the house. Because these materials are evocative of the past and often, of exotic places, woven and rustic willow furniture may even provide a subtle sense of roots, or suggest a fantasy. But psychology aside, there are a variety of ways you might incorporate wicker into your existing decor.

For instance, rush-bottomed seats around a table will add a country feel to the dining area or kitchen. Nostalgic wicker seating can be brought up to date and into the living room with a coat of paint and cushions in contemporary fabrics. Cantilevered chairs, caned in various ways, can be equally at home around a battered oak slab or a chrome and glass table. A willow table or chair can add spice to a Southwest-style room.

For homes full of antiques, there are William and Mary, Louis XVI, and other period pieces that feature caned chair seats and backs. (Fine cane seats have been made in England and France since the end of the seventeenth century, so there's no lack of options here.) Even in a minimalist modern decor, caned chairs designed by greats like Charles Rennie Mackintosh and Marcel Breuer, as well as those by contemporary artists, can make a striking statement. Even just an artfully woven basket, strategically placed, might be the perfect accent.

Wicker, cane, and willow offer plenty of possibilities, and we'll talk more about specific adaptations later in this chapter. But first let's look at the overall traditions, or styles, that shape our perceptions of these kinds of furniture; these would also be your keynotes if you chose to do an entire room in wicker, cane, or willow. Many of these ''genres'' overlap and borrow from one another, however, so this section is included only to stimulate your imagination and spark your creative thinking, not to lay down rules.

Plants and wicker work together naturally to create a sunny atmosphere. Right: Basket planters and a sisal mat help reinforce the light feeling of this room, while the cushions add color. Sunlight flows in freely, unobstructed by curtains.

A STYLE SOURCEBOOK

The Sun or Garden Room

Hearkening back to wicker's most recent incarnation as porch and garden furniture, this style celebrates the joys of nature indoors. In the early 1900s, people began to put glass in the windows of their porches to create sun parlors, then furnished these rooms with wicker, of course, and a variety of plants. As this trend gained momentum, manufacturers began producing matched sets of furniture to meet the growing demand for room groupings. (Up to this point, most wicker pieces had been unique, rather than ''matching.'')

Wicker furniture was nestled among the plant life—perhaps a settee, rocker, chairs, chaise, and card table. The furniture might be left in its natural state or painted white, brown, or dark green, but it usually boasted generous cushions that encouraged relaxation.

© R. Abraham/FPG International

© Peter Paige/design by Rona Levine

This style relies almost as much on plant life as it does on wicker, but you don't need a profusion of greenery. Sometimes just a few large plants in ornamental pots are enough to create the mood. Greenhouse-style windows or skylights make the burgeoning plant-life effect easy to achieve, though they can prove to be too much of a good thing: These windows often require blinds or awnings, because wicker, and some plants, suffer from too much sunlight. On the other hand, by choosing plants that will thrive in the light that's avail-able, and painting or papering the walls white or a light pastel color, any room in the house can use wicker to partake of this aura.

Trellises can be used as room dividers to further the garden atmosphere. Or apply painted latticework to the walls—and even the windows—to reinforce the garden motif. Wicker has a light, airy feel, evocative of warm, sun-drenched summer days; combined with plants that trail and climb in a rich profusion of green, a wicker-furnished garden room can be the ideal place to unwind.

Courtesy Polar Island Corp.

A room surrounded by windows (opposite page) looks great when furnished in wicker. White slat blinds help maintain the airy, sun drenched feeling, but can be adjusted to protect the interior from sun damage or can be closed altogether for privacy. Left: Large, colorful baskets are a mainstay of the tropicana style.

Tropicana Paradise

This style is similar to the sun or garden room, but partakes of exotica; rather than suggesting a garden, tropicana has more of a jungle feel. Grass mats, hammocks, large baskets, fabrics with bold Hawaiian or animal-skin patterns, dramatic uplighting through foliage, and furniture of rattan, bamboo, and wicker help define tropicana. A parakeet in a wicker bird cage or a parrot on a roost may serve as living accents, though carved wooden birds from Mexico do almost as well, and require less maintenance!

Sometimes tropicana may also incorporate nautical elements—sailcloth, nets, lobster-trap tables—to enhance the shipwrecked-on-a-desert-island fantasy. For a total treatment, people have gone so far as to paper their walls and ceiling with rush mats—even adapting them for use as curtains and window blinds.

Victorian Parlor

The Victorians loved wicker because they believed its serpentine curves soothed the spirit, while its fanciful forms stimulated the imagination. Wicker was well-suited to Victorian designs because it combined materials—rattan, reed, cane, bamboo strips, willow osiers—the way they combined styles—Rococo, Classical, Elizabethan, Chinese, Italian Renaissance.

While Victorians originally favored heavy, lavishly embellished wooden furniture, when plants, along with sunlight, began to invade their interiors, wicker came inside, too. Although antique chairs with caned backs and seats upholstered in velvet were well-

© John Deane

established denizens of the parlor, late in the nineteenth century all-woven furniture began to make an appearance as well, dressed up in a coat of paint. (In extreme cases, wicker was covered with gold leaf!)

Much of Victorian wicker featured motifs that combined elaborate curves and curlicues, shell forms, scrolls, garlands, and hearts. This complex-looking wicker was in turn combined with ornate, formal furnishings and sumptuous accessories. If this style feels right for you, *Victorian Splendor*, by Allison Kyle Leopold, details the current Victoriana revival and offers lots of ideas for adding amusing Victorian touches to the home.

Country Cottage

The recent country revival has been so complete that people talk about the difference between American country vs. French country vs. English country vs. Italian country, and don't forget Scandinavian country! Certainly, subtle variations do exist, but what these styles have in common is that they evoke the wholesome simplicity of the past. They preserve the artifacts of a cultural history and raise everyday objects to the level of high art.

Many people nurture secret dreams of living in a quaint, rose-covered cottage. Exposed

© William B. Seitz

If you like the look of Victorian wicker, but can't afford the originals, look at what manufacturers are offering in old-fashioned styles (opposite page). Although usually not as ornate as the real McCoy, modern adaptations have the advantage of being sold as matching sets or room groupings, whereas antiques were usually "one of a kind." Above: Cane furniture is right at home with wood floors, exposed beamwork, and the country look in general.

beamwork and brick, rag rugs on wooden floors, quilts, baskets, wood carvings, folk art, windowsill gardens, hutches, and handcrafted furniture are some of the accoutrements that help create a country atmosphere. Wicker armchairs and rockers, willow bedsteads, Amish or Shaker side chairs with cane seats are just a few of the possibilities available to add to any country decor; in fact, the variety of country-style cane, rush, or reed bottom chairs is fairly mind-boggling.

Country elements often show up in design schemes that aren't in any other way rurally inspired. For instance, a twig rocker can look perfectly at home in a contemporary living room. Maybe it's because natural materials and fine handcrafting have a universal appeal, but in any case, country doesn't have to mean kitsch. It can evoke the simple, less hurried lifestyle of the past, or it can be dressed up to grand style, evoking the country manor with elegant antiques, carefully chosen accessories, and luxurious fabrics.

The country style often partakes of rustic elements, such as the twig table pictured here (above). Right: Appalachian-style rustic has a playful, whimsical quality that makes it seem almost otherworldly, as if it were created in the forest by the "little people." Each piece is unique, since forms are suggested by the wood itself.

Rustic Retreat

Rustic differs from country in that it refers to a specific kind of furniture; these styles are often found cohabiting. Rustic furniture is characterized by twigs, sticks, branches, logs, and stumps that are made into furniture in as close to their original state as possible. It's a primitive style—forms of arms and legs are suggested by the wood itself, which might be anything from black walnut to oak—whatever the crafter can find to work with. Bent willow furniture falls into the Appalachian rustic category; this kind of "loopy" furniture has been made for hundreds of years, and sometimes the designs look almost Celtic.

The looser, irregular Appalachian style contrasts with the Adirondack style, which was derived from the carpentry tradition and so is more symmetrical and "straight." This style is younger than the Appalachian rustic—it's only been around for about one hundred years. With the rise of industrialization in the late nineteenth century there was a resurgence of interest in the outdoors; New York's Central Park stands as one monument to this preoccu-

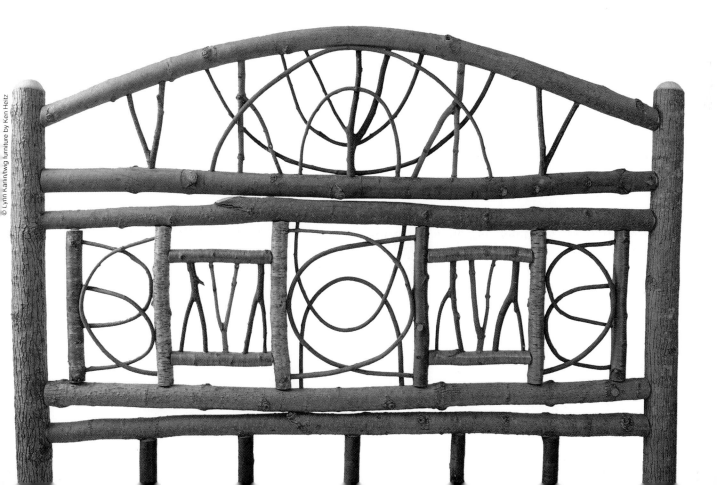

© Lynn Karlin/twig furniture by Ken Heitz

© William B. Seitz

pation with the natural world. As part of this back-to-nature movement, in the 1870s it became fashionable for wealthy Easterners to vacation at "camps" in the Adirondacks. These camps had all the comforts of home, but were built and furnished in a rustic style.

What has come down to us as Adirondack-style furniture is more strictly linear than Appalachian rustic. That's because much of the original Adirondack furniture was manufactured rather than handmade; but, even the hand-crafted Adirondack-style pieces were built according to the rules of carpentry, and thus are more "regular" looking. The Old Hickory Chair Company in Indiana, unfortunately no longer in existence, produced rustic-looking hickory wood furniture with woven rattan seats and chair backs that were standard furnishings for many of the great camps.

Appalachian rustic is more interpretive and intricate, more like a puzzle that's been put together. Since crafters take their cues from the wood itself, furniture possibilities are virtually endless—everything from birch branch chairs to cherry tree chaise lounges. Tree trunks and logs are often used for table bases and seating, and twigs can be used to make lamp shades, flowerpots, table bases, and wall units. (In Chapter Three you'll find instructions for making a log cabin table out of twigs.)

New York artist Daniel Mack, who handcrafts rustic furniture out of hardwoods, writes lyrically of his designs: "These chairs are cousins of the forest, made from saplings that wear their history on their bark. You see scars from browsing deer, broken branches, curious wood-peckers, and even the odd piece of buckshot. And in their graceful curves, you can still feel the relentless pursuit of sunlight."

The natural quality of rustic furniture blends easily with a variety of different decorating styles. Though informal and unpretentious, its unconventional use of materials has a certain bravura. A single piece can evoke the simple nobility of the past in an otherwise modern decor, while a room done entirely in rustic has an almost otherworldly quality—as if you'd become a hobbit and slipped into Middle Earth.

L*eft: "Loopy" bent willow furniture has been made in England since the 1700s, and similar designs have since been made in America by the Gypsies, Amish, and Native Americans. Crafters usually don't work from a set pattern, but build a piece branch by branch, alternating from side to side so the design is uniform.*

Oriental Den

Images of the mysterious Far East have captivated Western imaginations for more than two hundred years—silks and brocades, porcelain and cloisonné, the inscrutable Buddha, and bamboo and rattan furniture. Late in the seventeenth century, China opened Canton for trade with the West. When wealthy Chinese businessmen held parties in their homes, American and

L*acquered rattan furniture (below) has an unmistakably Oriental feel, especially when it's accessorized with vases, silky cushions, and Eastern artwork.*

Courtesy Ficks Reed Company

British businessmen were impressed with the fan-back rattan chairs they saw, and eventually bought them and shipped them home as novelty items.

Since rattan and bamboo originate in Asia, natural wicker furniture has an inherently Oriental feel. This has led to the popular misconception that most antique wicker is from Asia. While most rattan furniture was imported from Asia until the middle of the nineteenth century, after that it was manufactured in the United States. Much American-made wicker did imitate Chinese designs, however; for instance, the hourglass chair (so named because of the shape of its base) became popular in America after the Philadelphia Centennial Exhibition of 1876. (Hourglass chairs are now frequently referred to as Canton chairs.)

Oriental rugs, silk pillows, lacquered cabinets, bamboo screens, Chinese porcelain, cloisonné, parasol lamps or paper lanterns, statuary (including Buddha, of course), Canton chairs, large potted plants, and the colors red and black are characteristic of this genre. Rattan furniture, constructed from the poles rather than woven of cane or reed, and resembling bamboo, is often used in the manufacture of Chinese-inspired designs, but wicker works well in this scenario, too. (Note: As Oriental wicker frames are usually made of bamboo, they tend to be lighter than American-made frames, and thus cannot hold as much weight.)

Lacquer is a key ingredient of Oriental style—tables, screens, cabinets, and even walls are varnished to a high gloss; these lacquered objects are often decorated with bronze or gold stencilwork. Natural wicker furniture provides an interesting textural balance to the slick look of lacquer, while creating that aura of exoticism associated with the East.

Arab Tent

Strictly speaking, you'd find mainly pillows in an authentic Arab tent. But because many species of rushes and palms are indigenous to the Middle East, wicker has enjoyed widespread use at least since the time of Christ. (And, as mentioned previously, wicker furniture has been found in Egyptian tombs that predate Jesus by as many years as we postdate him!)

Evocative of Sheherazade's tales of the *Thousand and One Nights*, this style is enchanting and mysterious, even magical. Fabric covers the walls—sometimes it's even draped tentlike from the ceiling—either as wallpaper or in the form of hangings, rugs, or mats. Dhurrie or Persian rugs cover the floor, and embroidered silk or handwoven pillows abound. Brasswork pitchers and trays, boxes or low tables of carved wood supply additional accents. Simple wicker furniture, left unpainted, blends in naturally, adding to the rich assortment of textures.

Ancient trade routes encouraged borrowing among the Near- and Middle Eastern cultures, so this style has Indian and Turkish influences. And since the Moors occupied Spain for hundreds of years, Spanish accents might be appropriate as well.

Japanese Tea House

While the Chinese style described above is profusely decorated, the Japanese style is much more restrained and minimalist. The Japanese classically value a spare economy of furnishings: Tatami (rice straw) mats, floor cushions, shoji (rice paper) blinds, low tables, a futon (mattress), and perhaps a cabinet or trunk are just about all you'd find in any given room. The sole decoration might be a spray of flowers in a porcelain vase.

While most of us aren't ready to give up our furniture and sit on the floor, this sense of openness and space can be achieved by combining a few simple pieces of wicker or rattan furniture with key Japanese materials such as shoji and tatami. (Tatami mats can also be used as wall hangings.) The secret here is to choose streamlined furniture designs, and to reduce

Courtesy Wickerware Inc.

This simple rattan bookcase and the rattan picture frames with Japanese prints (above) help evoke an aura of the East in an otherwise Western room.

furnishings and accessories to a bare minimum. Artwork should also be minimal—a single flower arrangement illustrates the essence of this restraint.

Indian Bungalow

Visions of colonial India, oh yes sahib! Sisal mats or colorful woven rugs, wicker chairs, potted palms, and ceiling fans are mainstays of this style. Rattan came to Europe via India in the days of the British empire, and was popular from 1840 to 1900. As with Chinese style, rattan and other plants that yield materials for wicker are native to India, so there's a natural relationship here.

Indian handicrafts inject vitality to the scene: brightly colored cloth, sometimes embroidered or embellished with mirror work, is used for throw pillows and cushions; ceramic pots, tooled metalwork, intricately carved wooden screens, delicate teakwood end tables, and statuary of Indian gods and goddesses all conspire to create a dramatic atmosphere. Wicker and rattan furniture work organically in this environment, adding texture and solidity.

This high-backed wicker chair (below) *invokes visions of the Taj Mahal. Combining a chair similar to this one with potted palms and ceiling fans enables you to have an Indian-style decor in your home.*

© D.G. Arnold

This section has examined various interpretations of wicker, cane, and willow, as inspired by other times and places. Most of these styles share an element of romantic escapism, and many of them overlap. But once again, this section was included as a brainstorming aid, not to dictate any specific rules. Reinterpret these traditional themes to fit your own style and taste, combining your favorite elements. For example, a country home can get the Arab treatment by using a shirred fabric wall covering in an appropriate pattern, even quilts could be used, if you like the aura of the tent. Be creative in your adaptations, remembering that contrast is often the key to a supremely personal statement.

Wicker and rattan furniture work well together to create a casual, relaxed atmosphere. In this inventive scheme (right), pieces were painted different colors or left natural to create visual interest.

Pieces of the Puzzle

If you look around, you'll discover that wicker furniture is everywhere. It shows up in hairdressers' and doctors' waiting areas, in fast-food chains and expensive restaurants, in movies, and on TV. There's even been White House wicker: Mamie Eisenhower's wicker bridge table and John F. Kennedy's caned Adirondack-style rocker.

This furniture is available in a variety of styles, from elaborate Victorian scrolls and curlicues, to the understated elegance of a Bauhaus chair. And like anything, it can be taken to extremes. For instance, the mahogany toilet cabinet with caned back and lid that looks like a medieval throne, or the antique wicker fountains that inhabited Victorian interiors.

© Phillip H. Ennis

Before you can decide which kinds of wicker, cane, or willow will work in your house, you need to know what's available. The following is an alphabetical list of some possiblities.

ARMCHAIRS

BABY BUGGIES

BASKETS

BEDSIDE TABLES

BOOKCASES

BUFFETS

CABINETS

CHAISE LOUNGES

CLUB CHAIRS

COFFEE TABLES

COUCHES

CRIBS

DAYBEDS

DESKS

DRESSERS

END TABLES

FLOOR COVERINGS

HATRACKS

HEADBOARDS/FOOTBOARDS

Courtesy Lindal Cedar Homes, Inc.

In the late nineteenth century, wicker buggies were in such demand that one prominent manufacturer published a separate catalog of perambulators. Lately, some of these old buggies have been resurrected as decorative accents (above), thanks to both their sensuous curves and their rich woven texture. A wicker end table (right) can help make a small room look larger. It takes up very little space, and has an optical advantage as well: the lightweight weave doesn't "stop the eye" the way wood or another solid material does.

© Nancy Hill

© William B. Seitz

A wicker pet bed (left) looks perfectly at home in even the most elegant decor. White wicker has a fresh, clean look evocative of summertime, but you don't have to redo an entire room to achieve this effect. Sometimes just a couple of pieces— such as this mirror and end table (below)—can be like a breath of fresh air.

Courtesy Wickerware Inc.

HIGH CHAIRS

LAMPS

LOUNGE CHAIRS

MIRRORS

MUSIC STANDS

PET BEDS

PICTURE FRAMES

PLANT STANDS

PORCH SWINGS

ROCKING CHAIRS

SCREENS

SETTEES

SHELVES

SIDE CHAIRS

SOFAS

STROLLERS

TEA CARTS

TRUNKS

UMBRELLA STANDS

VANITY TABLES

WALL COVERINGS

WALL UNITS

WINDOW SHADES

© Charles Schneider/FPG International

A *rustic bent willow armchair (left) can act as an antidote to a high-stress, high-tech lifestyle, while providing its own brand of "twig chic." The basket chair, (above) characterized by its roundish shape and its fluid, unbroken lines, is one of the oldest wicker designs.*

Take It Sitting Down: Chairs

Available in every style imaginable—plus some you may never have dreamed of—chairs are probably the most versatile and adaptable pieces of the wicker puzzle. Integral to kitchens, dining rooms, living rooms, offices, or studies, and often used in bedrooms and bathrooms as well, designs run the gamut from rustic bent willow armchairs to tightly woven wicker club chairs, from simple Shaker rockers to Rococo side chairs.

Some of the most universal chairs (i.e., adaptable to many rooms and styles) are based on historical prototypes—variations of the medieval basket chair, for instance. Shaker-inspired designs, with their clean lines and exquisite craftsmanship, also work in a variety of decors. Modern classics include Michael Thonet's bentwood innovations of the late nineteenth century, as well as those derived from Marcel Breuer's tubular steel chair, created in 1925.

A Tisket, a Tasket, a Green and Yellow Basket

Woven furniture arose out of the basketry tradition, which may be the oldest human craft. A folktale explains the origins of the basket chair: Before the wheel was invented, the only way to cart wood or rocks was to strap two baskets on either side of a donkey. So one

day a tired worker took one of the baskets off the animal's back, turned it upside down, and sat on it. Voila—the basket chair was born!

That's apocryphal, of course, but the widespread use of wicker in the Middle Ages is well documented. A basket chair made of peeled willow twigs or woven rush was popular throughout medieval times and was called "the common chair" because it was used by the common people, while wealthy people sat on thrones of wood to show their status. (The joke was on them—elastic and lightweight, wicker furniture "gives" with body weight, as if you were sitting in a basket, so the common people were probably much more comfortable than the rich.) Various designs were popular throughout Europe; for instance, a sixteenth-century French basket chair was called a *guérite*, meaning sentry box. These chairs featured high, rounded backs that curved forward at the top to form a hood. By the seventeenth century the British had scaled down the backs, so the chairs resembled beehives more than they did sentry boxes.

In the mid 1850s, while Americans were producing ornate designs in wicker, the British were still making basket chairs. Some featured open latticework "skirts" as a base, and were called croquet chairs; both were popular in Britain thoughout the nineteenth century.

Above: Wicker chairs are extremely comfortable, because they "give" with the body's weight. In coordinated fabrics they make a design statement as well. The rocker is an American invention, first crafted by an anonymous colonist who joined a simple slat back chair to a pair of cradle rockers. The Shakers perfected the design by carefully curving the rockers for gentler motion. The simple lines of these Shaker rockers (opposite page) have an almost archetypal quality.

© Nancy Hill

Modern variations of the wicker basket chair abound, characterized by their fluid, unbroken lines. Woven in one piece on a Lloyd loom, the base resembles an inverted basket that flows up into a kind of half-basket shape comprising the back, seat, and arms. If the design features legs, they will be short and unobtrusive. Basket chairs work in traditional and modern decors.

"Hands to Work, Hearts to God" One of the many ways in which the Shakers expressed religious devotion was to make beautiful hand-crafted furnishings. They believed you should work as if you had a thousand years to live, and as if you were to die tomorrow. Simplicity was a high virtue, and everything they created was meant to be used and loved. By 1830, their chairs and rockers were sought after as the best in America. More recently, the poet Thomas Merton explained this fascination when he wrote, "The peculiar grace of a Shaker chair is due to the fact that it was built by someone capable of believing that an angel might come and sit on it."

© Bob Curtis

The Shakers were among the first to develop the rocking chair in the 1790s, and their Brumby rocker design is still imitated today. Originals of their simple ladder-back chairs with caned seats now sell for outrageous prices, though handcrafted Shaker-style reproductions or high-quality manufactured reproductions are more within reach. The clean lines of Shaker chairs have a timeless appeal—they look just as good in modern living environments as they do in more traditional settings.

The Industrial Revolution, According to Cane Chairs

German-born Michael Thonet is credited as being the first to combine elegant furniture design with mass production. He perfected the bentwood process wherein beechwood, softened by steam, is bent into curved shapes. In 1851, Thonet's furniture won the highest awards of the first World's Fair in London; this was also the year he began building a factory that would produce bentwood furniture for global distribution. Thonet subsequently manufactured furniture on a scale hitherto unknown in any industry, and printed multilingual catalogs so he could sell his designs all over the world. The chair designs he produced between 1860 and 1876, including the bentwood rocker and cafe-style side chair, are still popular today. Lightweight, elegant, and strong, Thonet designs, like Shaker chairs, have a classic simplicity that makes them compatible with a variety of decorating styles.

Bauhaus at Your House

In 1925, architect Marcel Breuer invented a chair that reinterpreted Thonet's bentwood design using a continuous tubular steel frame. Breuer was a student of the Bauhaus School, and he called this chair the Wassily after Wassily Kandinsky, who used it in the staff house on campus. Breuer wrote of his cantilevered design: "I considered such polished and curved lines not only symbolic of our modern technology, but actually

© Kent Oppenheimer

technology itself." Originally designed with a canvas seat and back, the chair was subsequently manufactured by Thonet Industries in various models that substituted woven cane for fabric. These are now known collectively as the Breuer chair.

Breuer chairs work especially well in small spaces because their "see-through" shape doesn't stop the eye, and thus makes a room seem larger. And although this is a modern design, when manufactured with natural cane or rush seats and backs, these chairs are at home in country and traditional decors as well as in contemporary ones.

Reclining in Style Settees, Sofas, and Chaises

These pieces are often used in conjunction with cushions and/or pillows, so that fabric color, texture, and pattern contribute significantly to the overall effect. Wicker styles range from sofas and chaises that are simple extensions of the basket chair, to Victorian fancy-work versions. Other designs feature rattan as an exposed framework for upholstery. Bent willow settees, on the other hand, make a strong statement with or without cushions.

Since they are relatively large, wicker sofas and chaises hold sway in a room. They can help

© William B. Seitz

The cantilevered Breuer chair (opposite page) is a modern design classic. Although they can be fabricated in everything from leather to sea grass, the cane and wood treatment shown here is probably most common. A bent willow settee (above) will add a touch of nostalgic whimsy to just about any room in the house—and don't forget the porch!

create a mood—be it rustic or tropical—in the blink of an eye. And since their woven surfaces are equally as attractive viewed from the back as from the front, they can also serve a practical function as a room divider. (Between the living and dining areas, for instance, or to separate the dining area from the kitchen.)

Modular sofas made of wicker are now widely available in various styles, and have the advantage of flexiblity. Also, many manufacturers offer complete living room groupings—sofas, love seats, and chaises, as well as lounge and club chairs, and coffee and end tables.

© Kent Oppenheimer

Lay Your Cards on the Table: Surfaces for All Occasions

Antique wicker card tables, smoking stands, tea carts, and bedside tables; a sleek modern dining room table featuring a glass top on a round wicker base; rustic log cabin end tables, circular woven coffee tables, rattan side tables. There's no shortage of options here. Some wicker tables are extremely whimsical; for instance, the elephant table, woven to resemble a pachyderm carrying a plate on its back, which comes in various sizes. Others are more formal—like antique wicker dining tables. And when you consider that large baskets, used upside down, can function as end tables, and that with a sheet of glass on top, a wicker trunk can serve as a coffee table, the possibilities just keep multiplying.

Sleep On It: Beds

Headboards and footboards, like everything else we've looked at so far, can be rendered plain or curlicued, in rustic willow or exotic rattan, in Bar Harbor- or Cape Cod-style wicker. Designs range from primitive to elegant, with a lot of room for interpretation in between. Many manufacturers sell entire matching bedroom suites that include bedside tables, vanities,

Courtesy Ficks Reed Company

$\mathcal{D}$on't be afraid to improvise—two wicker trunks topped with plexiglass can serve as a unique table, as pictured here (opposite page). Painted wicker in the bedroom (left) helps create an aura of romance. Wicker baskets and drawers are a beautiful way to store papers and supplies in a home office (below).

dressers, cabinets, armoires, and sometimes even desks. (We'll explore bedrooms in more depth later in this chapter.)

Everything in Its Place: Storage

Baskets, buffets, cabinets, dressers, etageres, shelves, tea carts, trunks, wall units, whatnots— wicker, cane, and willow offer practical as well as aesthetic help around the house. Wicker baskets in themselves are so useful that they're covered separately (see ''Basket Magic'' on page 46); many of these other pieces are executed in wrapped rattan (a hardwood frame is wound around with strips of rattan) rather than being woven.

© Nancy Hill

You'll find various styles of antique (or near-antique) storage furniture as well as modern manufactured versions, but one thing that stands unique is the wall unit. International Contract Furnishings (ITC) in New York sells (through designers only) "cupboard walls" as part of the Mutaro collection by Interlübke. The doors of this wall unit feature panels of fine canework; inside, it can be set up with a rod for hanging storage, outfitted with shelves, or equipped with drawers—in whatever configuration best serves your needs. While the cupboard wall was designed for bedrooms, it can be used in any room of the house.

Basket Magic

Even if your home is already well-furnished, you can incorporate baskets for a natural wicker accent. A basket of fruit or flowers can add just the right touch of warmth in an otherwise austere modern room; a formal living room full of French antiques will look friendlier if there's a basket of firewood on the hearth.

Baskets with lids are good for corraling things that you want to keep handy but out of sight: the kids' crayons, your jewelry or makeup, extra blankets or out-of-season clothes—in wicker trunks that can double as tables—and so on. (I personally use a dome-shaped lidded basket

Below: *Baskets are made all over the world, in every size, shape, and color imaginable. Baskets hanging from a beamed ceiling are a hallmark of the country style* (opposite page).

© William B. Seitz

© E.A. McGee/FPG International

© William B. Seitz

- In the kitchen, use baskets instead of drawers to store utensils, linens, and nonperishables like apples, pears, bananas, potatoes, and onions.

- Use a deep basket to carry ingredients from the refrigerator to your work center when you're ready to start cooking.

- In the bathroom, clean towels can be folded flat and stacked in a basket, or rolled up into tubes and stuffed in bouquet-style.

- Backup supplies of hand soap, toilet paper, and other toiletries can be stored in a lidded basket right in the bathroom.

- Small baskets of dried herbal potpourri will help freshen any room in your house.

- Why do you think they call them wastebaskets? Large woven baskets make great "circular files" for paper trash, and, lined with a disposable garbage bag, they work well in the bathroom.

- A split oak or wicker picnic basket will hold all your outdoor meal necessities—paper plates (and willow plate holders!), tablecloth, eating utensils, plastic cups, napkins—so all you need to do is pack the food and go.

to store bottles of colored ink for my fountain pens.) Or you can use baskets purely for decoration, by placing one beautiful basket as an objet d'art on a mantle or sidetable, or by hanging a profusion of them from a beamed ceiling for an informal, cozy look. For textural magic, mix different sizes and shapes of baskets made from split oak, rush, sea grass, and reed.

Baskets can be woven of just about any supple, pliant material, natural or manufactured—from pine needles to insulated copper wire. The following are a few ideas for using baskets throughout your home:

- Upside down, large baskets can be used as end tables, either as they are, or topped with glass or a metal tray. Smaller baskets are sometimes employed as lamp shades.

- If you knit, baskets display colorful yarns and knitting needles so they'll be working as accents even when you aren't working your creative magic with them.

- The sewing basket is a time-honored means of keeping needles and notions organized.

- If you like to write letters, use a basket to keep your stamps, pens, stationery, envelopes, and postcards all together, for one-step correspondence.

- Baskets can be used to keep magazines in an orderly group.

- A shallow basket can be used to corral the mail.

- Wicker laundry baskets wear longer and better than their plastic counterparts; plus, they're prettier!

- Empty baskets can serve as decorative objects in their own right. Unique designer baskets sell for hundreds, sometimes even thousands of dollars apiece.

- Store bottles of wine, bouquet-style, in a medium-sized basket.

- Baskets will hold houseplants of all sizes, from geraniums to ficus trees. (Just be sure to put a deep ceramic or plastic drainage dish inside, on the bottom, to avoid floods when you water the plants.)

- Likewise, an over-the-shoulder basket will keep beach and pool supplies in one convenient place in the summertime, so towels, sunscreen, beach balls, etc., are ready to go when you are.

- Small shallow baskets will display collections of rocks and shells and can do double duty as paperweights; larger baskets of such "earth treasures" will work as doorstops.

- Near the fireplace, a large basket will keep firewood neat, while a smaller one holds twigs for kindling.

- Place fruit in a basket while it ripens. This also makes a beautiful still-life centerpiece.

- Dried or silk flower arrangements work naturally in baskets, but a vase of fresh flowers can also be set inside a basket for a softer, more textural look.

- And finally, since it's better to give than to receive: baskets stuffed with treats make great presents. Home-baked goods are an old standby, or you can choose contents around a theme. For instance, "luxury bath" would include things like bubble bath, fancy soap, perfumed talc and body lotion, a loofah, a manicure kit, and silk flowers; "gourmet goodies" could include such delicacies as imported biscuits and jams, bags of specialty coffees and brightly colored tins of tea, a nutcracker and assorted nuts, caviar, smoked oysters, black olives, marinated artichoke hearts, and sun-dried tomatoes. Basket themes can be tailored to the recipient—if you know someone's special passion is Hawaii, say, or Porsche convertibles, you can shop around for appropriate items and arrange them in a decorative basket to show you care.

© Lynn Karlin

Courtesy Ficks Reed Company

Light and Reflections: Lamps and Mirrors

I once had a wicker lamp from Mexico that not only provided light but also cast beautifully patterned shadows on the wall, as the light filtered through the shade's woven slats. (Upside-down baskets can sometimes be used for lamp shades with similar effects.) So if you like "textural light," you'll love wicker lamps. Styles range from simple table lamps with tailored bases and tapered shades to floor lamps with bulbous fringed shades. Rustic lamp bases are built of twigs, log-cabin style, and feature twig or regular lamp shades.

Mirrors can sometimes be used to make a space look larger; when they're framed in wicker or rustic branches, they make a design statement as well. You'll find square, round, and oval wicker mirrors, as well as odd-shaped rustic ones. Sizes range from small mirrors for the wall to full length standing mirrors for the bedroom or bath.

Cover Ups: Window Shades, Wall and Floor Coverings

Cyrus Wakefield is known as the father of the American rattan industry because he was the first to manufacture this furniture on a large scale. As a young grocer in 1844, he noticed the huge piles of rattan on the docks in Boston, which, after serving as ballast on Chinese clipper ships, were discarded as trash. He experimented with the strange, flexible rods and quickly realized rattan's huge potential for furniture-making. He promptly quit the grocery and started a rattan business whose factories and warehouses eventually came to occupy ten acres of floorage.

Some manufacturers offer matching side tables and mirrors in rattan or wicker (opposite page). A woven mat (below) *can help create a cozier, "lived in" environment.*

© Jeff McNamara/James Gostee III, stylist

In 1856 Wakefield's ingenuity was tested again. The Opium Wars had cut off his supply of rattan, so he looked around for ways to use the waste that was lying around in stock. With help from his assistant William Houston, Wakefield developed a process of spinning rattan shavings into a yarn, which could then be woven into mats. The mats in turn could be used as floor coverings, or window blinds.

Today, more than 130 years later, Wakefield's innovation still looks modern. Whether they're woven from rattan scraps, rice straw, sisal, or any other natural material, these floor coverings lend a warm, light quality to any room. (Some mats can be adapted to use as wall coverings and curtains as well.)

Likewise, walls papered in grass cloth give rooms a light, airy feel, though in general grass cloth has a more luxurious effect than fiber floor coverings. Loosely woven of various grasses or other vegetable fibers, grass cloth has a lustrous sheen and subtle texture that makes it almost sensuous. But, while grass cloth will hide a multitude of sins—cracks, pits, and bad walls in general—its drawback is seamy: it comes in narrow rolls like wallpaper, and the fibers occupy so much space that the seams have a tendency to show.

To get around this problem, Conrad Imports of San Francisco sells (through designers only)

© Ralph Mercer/FPG International

*W*oven fiber placemats (above) *add a touch of warmth to any meal. Woven window blinds* (right) *are versatile enough to work well in just about any decorating scheme—from formal to casual, and everything in between.*

woven wall coverings called suma weaves, which come in nine-foot (three-meter) rolls. That way the wall can be wrapped in one continuous sheet, effectively eliminating seams. Suma weave is made from either straw and jute or from split reed and jute. Since jute can be dyed, suma weaves are available in black, tea brown, white, emerald, and beige, as well as in natural tan.

Window treatments range from simple pull-down bamboo or reed blinds to custom woven shades of reed, grasses, flax, abaca, and/or arrowroot. The main difference is that bamboo shades have cut edges on the sides, while loomed fiber blinds have smooth, continuous edges. But all of these window treatments, from the least expensive to the most luxurious, filter sunlight without blocking it out so you can

© Kent Oppenheimer

still see the view from between the slats. This visual advantage turns into a liability at night, however, when peeping toms can reverse the principle and get an eyeful of your lighted house from between those same slats. This may not matter in the living room, but woven fiber blinds in bedrooms should always be equipped with an independently controlled blackout shade.

W*hen woven blinds are used in a room where privacy is an issue (below), such as the bath or bedroom, they should always include a blackout shade. This heavy-core wicker livingroom set (right) helps unify all the diverse elements of the room. (Heavy-core wicker is made of larger reed, and thus is even stronger and more durable than regular wicker.)*

© Steve Hogben/FPG International

© Steve Hogben/FPG International

PUTTING IT ALL TOGETHER

So far in this chapter we've looked at materials, overall styles, and individual pieces of furniture. Now it's time to take a walk through the house, to decide where wicker, cane, and willow will work most to your advantage.

Modern eclecticism holds that beautiful things can always live happily together, even if they're from different time periods and all corners of the globe. If you subscribe to this model, you've probably experienced the special thrill that comes when your search pays off and you discover various pieces that seem to just belong together. On the other hand, if you've heretofore been rather cautious, sticking safely within the parameters of a particular style, allow yourself to entertain other possibilities. Think about the wicker, cane, or willow pieces that most appeal to you, and look for ways you could incorporate them into your existing decor. You may surprise yourself with your own daring and come up with innovations the designers haven't even thought of yet!

Living Rooms

An entire living room done in wicker is like a breath of fresh air. Whether the wicker is painted or left natural, it contributes to an open, outdoorsy mood. There's a design truism that color helps create relationships between form, pattern, and texture in a room, so this ''natural vs. painted'' choice is important.

Natural wicker works especially well with earth tones and shades of red and blue, but the

Courtesy Palecek

color combinations for painted wicker are limited only by your imagination. The cushions can be used to contrast or complement a given scheme, with fabric possiblities ranging from solid colors or delicate patterns to bold prints, from sailcloth to chintz. Throw pillows add yet another dimension: you could choose quiet pastel accents or go for striking Guatemalan prints, depending on the room. Different cotton prints, mixed and matched around a color scheme, are another popular way to coordinate cushions and throw pillows—these prints can appear in the curtains and wall coverings as well.

Manufacturers offer sleek, basket-style wicker groupings that include sofas, love seats, club or lounge chairs, ottomans, coffee tables, side tables, and lamp tables. Sometimes cushions are sold separately, but more often they're part of the piece, so if you love the furniture design but aren't thrilled with the fabric, you may decide to cover (or replace) the cushions.

If you prefer the more whimsical look of old-fashioned wicker, you may want to hunt for some authentic antique pieces at flea markets and garage sales. (In which case, you should study Chapter Two for tips on how to evaluate wicker.) Your chances of finding an entire matched living room set are next to nil, and if you do, it will be pricey. So if you like antique fancywork, but have a fetish for matched sets, investigate the reinterpretations of old styles that are being manufactured today.

Even if you aren't about to redo your entire living room in wicker, consider adding a well-chosen piece or two. A conversation grouping of different colored, tight-weave armchairs can work like sculpture in a space; coordinated cushions, wicker armchairs, and rockers can add a nice textural contrast to your upholstered furniture. A rush-bottomed chair could help balance a side table; a caned chair might be the perfect complement to your desk. A willow or log cabin-style side table—or even just a grapevine wreath above the mantle, or a basket of firewood on the hearth—may add just the right touch of rusticity to an otherwise purely modern (or traditional) decor.

Rattan furniture has an Oriental quality that's often emphasized, but it can adapt to a variety of styles. Rattan's exotic elegance allows it to hobnob with rare antiques, but it can also look down-home country if the mood is right. Cushions have alot to do with it, as does the frame construction—like wicker, rattan styles range from the streamlined to the ornate. And it's perfectly feasible to outfit an entire living room in rattan, since manufacturers offer groupings similar to those in wicker: sofas, coffee tables, armchairs, etc.

© Steve Hogben/FPG International

Opposite page: *The same wicker grouping can be dressed up or down by your choice of fabric. Using a key fabric judiciously throughout a room is a time-honored trick for pulling a space together* (above).

© Kent Oppenheimer

Bent willow furniture is usually used as an accent in the living room rather than as a predominant style, though by carefully selecting your pieces you could create a "matched" grouping without too much trouble and most willow crafters would certainly make one to order. Willow rockers, chairs, settees, and tables are right at home in country or Southwestern decors, and can add a playful touch to traditional or contemporary interiors as well.

Kitchens and Dining Rooms

Wicker works especially well in combination kitchen/dining areas because it's more formal than most kitchen furniture, yet it's cozy, too. Even in a house with a formal dining room, families often eat their meals in the kitchen, or will entertain friends here casually, as they cook, so "the heart of the home" may be living up to its name.

First off, realize that chairs don't necessarily have to match. If you're into antiques, you know that one good chair is easy to find, but a matched set is going to be expensive. One option is to combine the antique chair with a good set of compatible reproductions. A bolder solution would be to put wicker armchairs at the ends, with wooden benches or caned chairs at the sides of a plain oak or pine table. Or you could substitute Adirondack-style armchairs at the ends, with Shaker-style side chairs around the table. If you're really daring, you might even use quirky willow chairs around a sleek, glass-topped table. In any case, brightly colored cushions, coordinated with the table linens, will help pull everything together, festively.

Stools with cane or rush seats will create an informal eating area next to a work island or bar. For a table near a wall, a settle with a rush or cane seat, left natural or painted, serves well for seating. For a more contemporary look, consider bentwood cafe chairs or Breuer chairs around a glass-topped or wood slab table.

Whether they're left bare or partially covered by a rug, wooden floors enhance the look of wicker, cane, and willow furniture. This is especially true in sunny rooms, where light plays up the color relationship between these natural materials.

Cane-bottomed stools (opposite page) *along a bar create an informal eating area. A set of cane chairs add grace and style to kitchen dining* (below).

© E.A. McGee/FPG International

Courtesy Ficks Reed Company

Although all of the ideas above will work in dining rooms, if you like a more formal atmosphere for entertaining, check out what manufacturers are doing with rattan and wicker. Tables are usually pedestal based, with glass tops, or wrapped rattan, while chair designs vary dramatically, in both rattan and wicker. Many dining room sets also include buffets and tea carts. Of course you aren't limited to any one set; you can substitute a different table and use wicker or rattan chairs, or use a wicker-based table with upholstered chairs. And don't forget caned chairs, where styles range from rush-seated Mexican ladder-backs to reproductions of Louis XVI cane-worked side chairs. You could adapt the mix-and-match chair idea to this more formal setting, using upholstered dining arm chairs at the ends, with rattan or wicker side chairs.

Even if you're perfectly happy with your present dining room and kitchen furnishings, there are lots of woven accessories that will help spice up these environments.

A wicker dining room has an air of relaxed elegance (opposite page). With different accessories, it can evoke the langorousness of summer in the deep South, or the rugged camplike feel of the North woods. A wicker basket is both beautiful and useful; in the kitchen they can hold everything from dish towels to onions (above).

- Willow serving baskets, paper plate holders, and small baskets for chips and pretzels are great for informal entertaining and can be a civilizing influence on family snacks as well, (e.g., people will use a chip basket instead of munching right out of the bag).

- Woven maize or willow trivets lend an earthy elegance to casual table settings.

- Everybody knows that baskets are old hands at serving bread, rolls, and muffins, but did you realize they can also be adapted to hold hors d'oeuvres?

- A log cabin planter full of zinnias or snapdragons can be used as a centerpiece to add zest to a country, traditional, or contemporary decor.

- Bamboo or willow trays are perfect for serving meals indoors or out.

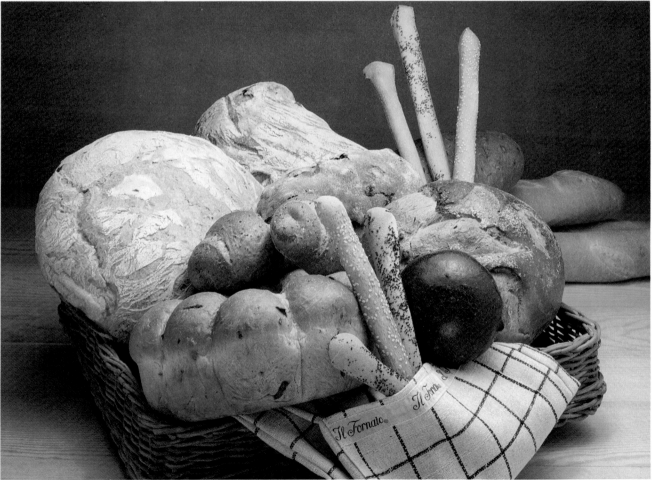

© Brian Leatart

For more ideas on how baskets can be used throughout your home, refer back to "Basket Magic" on page 46.

Bedrooms

When I was eleven my best friend Aliceanne had what I thought was an absolutely dreamy pink bedroom with white wicker headboard, nightstand, and dressing table. But her mother had decorated the room without consulting her, and Aliceanne hated it. She made sculptures out of rusty junk (which weren't allowed in her room, of course), and on rainy days she'd throw worms at the boys, so obviously that bedroom was just too prissy for her. Maybe if the wicker had been left unpainted, or if the room had been any color but pink . . . .

The point is, for an unabashed romantic revel, it's hard to beat white wicker in the bedroom. Combined with ruffles, lace, ribbons, chintz, and delicate floral prints in pink, peach, violet, yellow, or robin's egg blue, accented with pillows, fresh cut flowers, or ferns on stands, wicker can turn your bedroom into a romantic hideaway.

Matching the bedspread and curtains with coordinated wallpaper has been popular since the middle of the nineteenth century, and this old trick is still being reinterpreted daily by

Courtesy Amish Country Collection

The bread basket (opposite page) *is an old standby because it serves its purpose so beautifully. A handcrafted rustic bedstead* (above) *can work like a sculpture in space, and a room thus furnished will require little else in the way of decoration.*

contemporary designers, who will also coordinate the sheets and pillowcases for a total look. Combined with wicker furniture and accents like needlepoint or appliquéd throw pillows, a linen tablecloth over the nightstand, or an embroidered silk shawl draped over a chair, any bedroom can become charmingly nostalgic.

For a more rugged look, use natural wicker with earth tones—browns, beige, taupe, bronze, clay red—and plain, tailored bedspreads and curtains. (You might want to replace the curtains with woven blinds.) Patchwork quilts look wonderful with both natural and painted wicker, as well as with rustic bedsteads, which are pretty darn rugged themselves. Rattan bedroom suites often come in fairly strong, simple styles, though there are lighter, and more intricate, designs as well.

Willow and wicker can be combined in the bedroom, or you may choose to use only one piece: a wicker trunk to store blankets or sweaters at the foot of the bed, or a willow nightstand, for instance. A caned chair next to a table can serve as an impromptu desk for writing letters or paying bills; a wicker armchair or loveseat will help create a sitting-room atmosphere. Situated by a window, a bentwood or Adirondack-style rocker might become a favorite place to immerse yourself in a novel.

Courtesy Wickerware Inc.

© Dick Luria/FPG International

Bathrooms

Bedrooms aren't the only places being lent the air of a small sitting room. Nowadays, armchairs are showing up in bathrooms as well, and a lot of them are made of wicker. I'm not exactly sure who does all the sitting in this most private of rooms, but if you like to chat or relax in the loo, maybe you could use a wicker chair in there. (You could always use the chair to throw your clothes over while you bathe.)

Wicker has long been the material of choice for clothes hampers, as it supplies natural ventilation. You can also use smaller baskets in the bathroom to store towels, cosmetics, and extra bars of soap. You might even use a basket for magazines (or a wicker magazine rack), if this is where you catch up on your reading.

Baskets are great for storing towels decoratively (below) *and make them easily accessible when they are needed.*

© Dick Luria/FPG International

Left, top: Wicker organizers work equally well in the *boudoir, bedroom, or bath. Wicker chairs work well in the bath* (left, bottom), *as they thrive on moisture.*

Baby's and Children's Rooms

Around the turn of the century, everything a baby could possibly need was made in wicker: high chairs, strollers, buggies, cradles, and bassinets. Baby buggies were in such great demand in the 1880s that the Heywood Brothers and Company issued a separate trade catalog devoted solely to perambulators. Aside from bassinets and the occasional buggy, however, few of these things are maufactured today. You can still find them, if you haunt antique shops and flea markets, though I should think a wicker high chair would be a nightmare to keep clean.

But how about wicker furniture for *you* in the baby's room? An armchair, or better yet, a rocker, could be a special, comfortable place to

Courtesy Pella/Rolscreen Company

Courtesy Laura Ashley

Left: *Various wicker styles were combined in this girl's room to create a light, feminine atmosphere. Besides being beautiful this large wicker basket (above) provides a home for wayward dolls and stuffed animals.*

spend time with your child. Once you've picked the style of rocker that helps create the atmosphere you're after (remembering that rockers range from Shaker purity to Victorian splendor), be sure to test-drive a few. A lovely design that you aren't comfortable sitting in will defeat the whole purpose.

When it comes to kids, remember my friend Aliceanne and ask their opinions before you make major changes, since they're the ones who're going to have to live with it. Though who knows, maybe your little girl will swoon (as I would've) if offered a frilly pink and white wicker bedroom.

Although any of the above ideas for bedrooms can be adapted for children's rooms, a rustic log bunk bed might give kids who share a room some coveted privacy, plus it's sturdy enough to withstand almost anything.

If your kids are still pretty little, child-sized chairs are available in rustic and cane-bottom styles. And of course baskets can be used to store everything from stuffed animals to marbles to shoes. (If you put a large basket on the closet floor, kids can just throw their shoes in when they take them off. Putting shoes on again requires a little hunting, but meanwhile the closet floor stays neat.)

Porches, Patios, and Pools

Now that wicker and willow have made themselves at home in the house, it's easy to forget that for years the porch and patio were their unchallenged domain. The ornate settee was the most popular outdoor piece, but you could find everything from fern stands to porch swings on a typical Victorian veranda.

But rather than using wicker to the exclusion of all else, the modern spirit of eclecticism allows us to combine it with any number of other outdoorsy elements: wrought-iron patio furniture, humorous willow chairs, ceramic urns full of plants and flowers, and rugged hardwood furniture, for instance. Porches and patios are casual by nature, so a playful treatment is perfectly apropos here.

© William B. Seitz

Rattan's tough, glossy outer peel makes it very water-resistant, and thus well suited to outdoor use. With a coat of polyurethane, it's virtually impenetrable. (Rattan is so strong, in fact, that Asians use it to make rope for cables on moorings, and even for suspension bridges!) It would probably be much better than wicker to use poolside, for instance, from a maintenance standpoint.

UNIVERSAL WICKER

The extraordinary versatility of furniture made from wicker, cane, and willow lets it live happily in a variety of different settings. So whether your home is country, traditional, contemporary, or eclectic, you can find wicker that will work to your advantage, pieces that are compatible in style, color, and scale with the rest of your furnishings. Or perhaps a new favorite will inspire you to redo the entire room, building a scheme around that one piece. This can be a supremely satisfying experience because, ultimately, your home doesn't just represent your style. It represents you.

© Kent Oppenheimer

*B*ent willow chairs (opposite page) *have a rugged, earthy look that works well outdoors. These sinuous rattan lounge chairs (left) have a sleek gracefulness that coordinates easily with other styles of outdoor furniture.*

© Nancy Hill

Chapter Two

HOW TO BUY AND CARE
FOR WICKER, CANE, AND
WILLOW

If you frequent flea markets or garage sales, you've probably noticed a lot of wicker that has seen better days. Or maybe you've found pieces without noticeable flaws, but were unsure whether they were worth the asking price. Not all new wicker is created equal, either. You need to know how to judge craftsmanship.

Like Oriental rugs, good wicker can be very expensive, but quality and price vary widely. This chapter will teach you how to evaluate both old and new furniture to help insure that you get the most for your money. You'll also learn how to care for wicker, so you can protect and enjoy your investment for years to come.

WICKER WORKS

In order to evaluate wicker intelligently, you need to be familiar with some basic terminology. The following section provides a brief review of materials, and a basic working vocabulary that will help when you're ready to judge specifics.

The Right Stuff

As explained in Chapter One, wicker derives from many different materials, but it is most often woven of reed (from the pith of the rattan plant), or of a synthetic material called fiber rush, made of twisted paper. Glue is used as sizing to help stiffen fiber rush, and sometimes a wire in the center of each strand lends additional strength.

There is nothing wrong with fiber rush as long as you know what you're buying. Today fiber rush is used mainly to make bathroom hampers, though some furniture is manufactured from it as well. (I've seen chairs and bedroom suites.) In the past, however, it was used to make just about everything, so you should definitely be able to identify fiber rush if you intend to purchase old wicker.

One way you can tell the difference between a reed and fiber rush is to look underneath the piece. Diagonal grooves and ragged ends distinguish the twisted paper of fiber rush from natural reed fibers. Sometimes old chairs and tables can be tagged as fiber rush by their braided legs. (Since it can't be rolled like reed, manufacturers often used braids on fiber rush pieces instead.) Also, if you look closely, you'll see that fiber rush has little ribs, like twined rope, whereas reed is smooth.

If you're not sure whether something is made of fiber rush or not, ask. If the owner doesn't know, there are ways to check, but get permission first. The first involves snipping off a small strand of wicker where it won't show: from the back of a chair skirt, for instance. (Pick a spot where the paint isn't piled on too thickly, as this may interfere with the results.) Then try to unravel the strand; if it untwists, it's fiber rush. Or you can immerse a piece of the fiber in water. After about twenty minutes, small air holes will begin to show up on reed, whereas fiber rush will disintegrate. In fact, the main difference between these two materials is that fiber rush must *never* be soaked in water in preparation for repairs, as reed is, because fiber rush dissolves when wet.

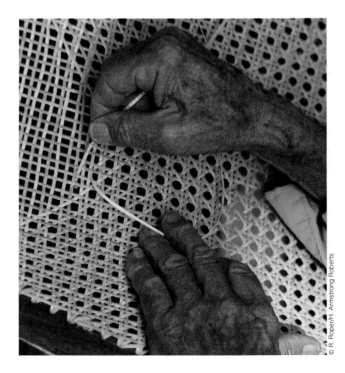

© R. Roper/H. Armstrong Roberts

Raising Cane

Cane, as you know, comes from the tough outer coat of the rattan vine. Once stripped from the vine, cane is machine-cut into various lengths and thicknesses; it's then used for cane seats or to wrap and bind joints on wicker and rattan furniture.

Cane seats can be made in either of two ways: strips of cane are handwoven on the chair frame, or a prewoven sheet of cane webbing is pressed into place, then fastened. The chair design determines the treatment: If

*T*he characteristic latticework of cane seats is created by weaving strands of reed through drilled holes in the chair frame (below left). Crafters use pegs to hold individual strands of reed tightly in place until the piece is completely woven (below). Then each individual strand is "tied off" and the pegs are removed.

© Lucian Niemeyer/LNS Arts

Courtesy H.H. Perkins/photo by Ray DeFrancesco

Prewoven cane webbing (above) is used to reseat cane
chairs that have a groove around the seat opening instead of
drilled holes. This Bar Harbor-style wicker chair (opposite
page, left) is executed in a loose, open weave; by necessity, the
seat is more tightly woven. Chairs similar to this sleek basket
design (opposite page, right) are machine woven on a Lloyd
loom. The advent of this new technology in 1917 made tightly
woven Cape Cod-style wicker more affordable.

there is a groove around the outside edge of
the seat, the chair takes prewoven cane; if there
is a ring of small holes instead of a groove, the
chair must be hand-caned. (You'll find instructions for recaning a chair in Chapter Three.)

In the past, seats were also woven from rush,
but this is almost a lost art in the United States,
although it's still done extensively in Europe.
Rush work is time consuming and hard on your
hands, plus it requires a lot of preparation: The
dried rush must be soaked, wrapped in paper,
and left for days, then resoaked and twisted as
the seat is constructed—and often it's difficult
to obtain in the first place. (The drought of
1988, for instance, made that year's rush har-
vest almost nonexistent, and many of the
plants that did survive to be harvested suc-
cumbed to mold in storage.) Fiber rush is often
used instead, because it's easily obtainable
and simple to work with.

Wicker Weaves

As you may recall, Bar Harbor-style wicker
features an extremely loose weave, so that
there are large gaps between the latticework;
Cape Cod-style, on the other hand, is more
closely woven.

But the look of wicker is also affected by the
size of the reed used to weave the piece. Reed

sizes range from $3/64$ to $5/8$ of an inch (.01 centimeter to 1 centimeter). (Or, if you're like me and have trouble visualizing measurements, they range in size from the diameter of angel hair spaghetti to that of a thick stalk of asparagus). The size of the reed has an impact on the durability of a piece as well. The larger the reed, the sturdier the piece tends to be because bigger reed is not as likely to split or break. This larger, heavy-core wicker has a more masculine look, and may also tend to look more modern, while the delicate fibers have a more dainty, traditionally feminine, look.

© Sandra Dos Passos

Courtesy Lloyd/Flanders Industries Inc.

WICKER FURNITURE CONSTRUCTION GLOSSARY

The following definitions explain some basics of wicker furniture construction; often, these are things to look for when evaluating wicker, cane, and willow. Once you understand these basics, you'll be better able to judge quality, as well as to estimate repairs accurately, when you encounter damaged wicker.

BRACES

Pieces of metal or wood often used in the corners to help support the frame of large wicker pieces such as chaises, sofas, and armchairs.

BRAID

A decorative strip of woven strands sometimes used around the edges of chairs or tables. The braid on old pieces is often damaged, but is usually quick and simple to repair. (If braid is used on the legs of a table, the piece is probably fiber rush.)

HAND CANING

Strands of cane are woven through holes in the frame by hand, to form a pattern. Usually executed in a basic open weave, other traditional designs include spiderweb, star of David, sunray, and sunburst.

OPEN WEAVE

A style of wicker characterized by widely spaced spokes and few weavers, typified by Bar Harbor wicker.

OPEN WORK

Areas without weavers where only the spokes show.

PAIRING WEAVE

Found in open-work furniture, a pair of reeds are twisted horizontally to help hold the spokes in place, as well as to add strength.

PRESSED CANE

Cane that's been machine woven into sheets that can then be pushed into a routed groove around the edge of a chair seat, and held in place with spline.

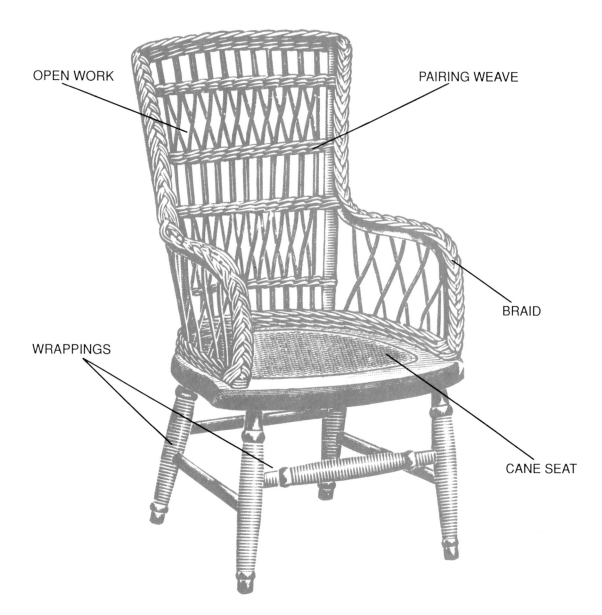

OPEN WORK

PAIRING WEAVE

BRAID

WRAPPINGS

CANE SEAT

Courtesy Dover Publications, Inc.

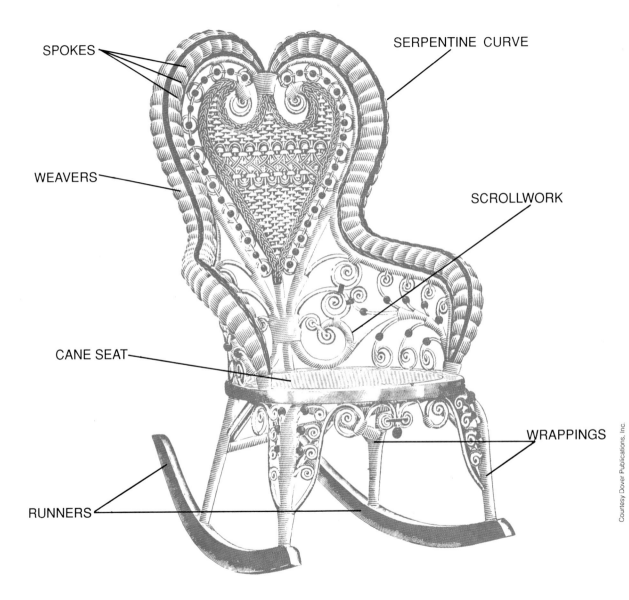

SPOKES

SERPENTINE CURVE

WEAVERS

SCROLLWORK

CANE SEAT

WRAPPINGS

RUNNERS

Courtesy Dover Publications, Inc.

RUNNERS

The curved pieces of wood on which a rocking chair rests.

SCROLLWORK

Common on the arms, backs, and legs of older pieces, scrollwork ranges from broad loops to complex curlicues, and often resembles curling vines. Highly decorative and subject to damage, it's a main component of the Victorian look.

SERPENTINE

Often found on chair arms and backs, the serpentine line is another frequent feature of Victorian pieces. The wicker is woven into a convex curve, creating a hollow area underneath.

SKIRT

The woven material covering the front of a chair beneath the seat.

SLATS

To help relieve stress on the woven material, wicker seats often have small pieces of wood nailed to the frame or held in place by dowels on the underside.

SPLINE

A thin strip of triangular reed that holds the pressed cane in the routed groove around the chair seat; spline is glued into place.

SPOKES

Vertical strands of reed or fiber rush that form the basis for the weaving.

WEAVERS

Reeds or fibers that are woven under and over the spokes, horizontally. The weaving of these fibers create the wicker pattern.

Something Old or Something New?

One of your first decisions is whether to buy antique or contemporary wicker. This will be influenced partially by the style you prefer, but other factors may play a part as well. For instance, do you enjoy the thrill of the chase? If one of your favorite pastimes is haunting flea markets and estate auctions, old wicker is a natural choice because you're already putting yourself "where the action is." On the other hand, if you are a no-nonsense type who wants instant results once you've made a decision, the process of tracking down the exact old pieces you have in mind may feel too much like a wild-goose chase. You'd probably be happier

© Daniella Jo Nilva

collecting some contemporary manufacturers' catalogs to find what you want or doing some window shopping, and then purchasing your furniture new.

If you're in the market for willow furniture, your search will be a little more specialized. It was made in England as early as the 1700s, and subsequently built by gypsies, the Amish, Native Americans, and Shakers. Although some antique dealers maintain collections of rustic twig furniture, including willow, the pickings tend to be slimmer because this style was not as universally accepted as wicker. Bent willow furniture is rapidly gaining popularity today, however, so there are individual crafters and cottage industries devoted to this art. (Ask around in your area and check out craft fairs—you may be able to find a local artist.)

Before spending any money on wicker or willow furniture, old or new, have a fairly good idea of what you want. Also think about where and how you intend to use the piece: Will it get daily, occasional, or seasonal use, or will it be purely decorative? The answers to these questions will help you make intelligent buys. For example, if a chair will be used daily (at the dining table, for instance), you should buy the best you can afford; if the chair will be used only on the porch in summer, your quality standards need not be so stringent.

Courtesy Daniel Mack Rustic Furnishings/photo by Bobby Hanson

Opposite page: *If you set your heart on an antique rustic settee like this one, be prepared to enlist a dealer's help in tracking it down. A rustic chair like this one* (above) *is definitely one of a kind, and performs an aesthetic as well as a practical function.*

Always Test-Drive Furniture

No matter how old or young a piece may be, if it will be used with any regularity, make sure it's sturdy and comfortable. Sit on sofas and chairs to make sure they don't wobble or sway, and that they offer enough support. Does the back conform to your shape, or do you feel forced into it? Shift your weight around to see if there are support bars or decorative braids that dig into you awkwardly. Wiggle the arms of chairs to check for solid construction. Check the backward angle of rockers—is it comfortable or too extreme? Rock in the chair for a little while to see if the runners move smoothly on the floor, without jerks or jolts.

As for tables, shake them gently to see if they're sound; place a lamp or other object on top to see how much weight they will bear; lamps should stand up straight, without wobbling. Pull out drawers and make sure they slide back in smoothly.

The main test for any piece of wicker furniture is to grasp it firmly with both hands, bearing down slightly, and shake it. Does it feel solid? It shouldn't wiggle much, and if you have the slightest doubt about its stability, pass it by. Life has enough uncertainties without having to worry about whether your furniture will support you.

Always make sure you test drive your purchase before buying it (above). Sitting in a chair will allow you to discern how sturdy it is. With tables, do the "shake test"—gently bear down on it and shake to see if it is sturdy. Old wicker furniture is available in every possible condition, from mint to hopeless. With a little practice, you can learn to recognize a bargain (opposite page).

 Buying Old Wicker

Although antique wicker is generally better constructed than most modern reproductions, both in framework and weaving, prices have doubled or tripled in the last decade. And as wicker becomes more and more popular, prices continue to rise. Single pieces now sell for anywhere from $100 to $2,000 (£60 to £1,200); six-piece sets can run as 'high as $8,000 (£5,000). Condition is a key factor in price.

© B. Vogel/H. Armstrong Roberts

If your heart is set on antique wicker, but you're on a limited budget, you'll have to be wily. By learning to tell the difference between superficial and serious structural damage, you may be able to pull off a coup. Sometimes those old pieces that look moth-eaten are actually great bargains—they can be restored to

© Jeff McNamara

their former beauty and usefulness with very little bother and expense. You may even be able to do it yourself.

But be cautious! Other times, a piece that seems in near-perfect condition can have serious structural problems that will be impossible, or very expensive, to repair. For instance, let's say you find an old Bar Harbor-style chair at a great price. Its only flaw is a couple of broken spokes in the back. One or two spokes are simple to replace, but when you look closely you notice the chair was woven of fiber rush and the broken spoke doesn't have a wire core. This tells you that the fiber rush spokes aren't really strong enough for the weight-bearing job they were designed to fulfill—and eventually *all* the spokes would need to be replaced. Thus, the chair is no bargain.

Also, just because wicker is old doesn't necessarily mean it's good. In addition to some downright inferior pieces that were manufactured in the past, so-so versions of popular designs were also sold. Check for labels—Wakefield Rattan Company and Heywood Brothers are some of the best—but even if the piece is unmarked, some old catalogs still exist that may help you identify it. (*The Heywood Brothers and Wakefield Co. Classic Wicker Furniture: Complete 1898–1899 Illustrated Catalog*, published by Dover Books, is a good place to start.)

Some antique pieces were not really designed for hard, consistent use. For instance, beginning in the 1880s, elaborate wicker chairs were a standard prop in many photography studios. They were often asymmetrical and ornate, but because these chairs were never occupied for more than a few minutes, they were made to be pretty rather than practical, and aren't really very comfortable. A photographer's chair would serve well as a seat to display dolls or stuffed animals, but humans will suffer if forced to sit in one for very long.

The best antique wicker was handmade in the United States, and features a heavy, hardwood frame. The corners of larger pieces are braced, and joints are fastened with hand-wound cane bindings. Avoid pieces with too many curlicues and those that look too new; sometimes unscrupulous people will try to pass off a modern reproduction as the authentic article.

The most valuable antiques are still in their natural state: they haven't been modified in any way. Natural Victorian wicker, for instance, is worth twice as much as its painted equivalent. Likewise, a piece that's been damaged won't be as valuable, though if the repairs conform with the materials and construction methods of the original, it won't knock as much off the resale price as if the repairs were made without regard for these factors. Thus, to help

Opposite page: *Sometimes slightly damaged furniture can be used as is—note the loose and broken runners in the skirt of this chair. On the other hand, a simple repair would make this chair as good as new. This photographer's chair (above) is typical of those found in studios around the turn of the century; they were beautiful, but very uncomfortable.*

© Jim Widess

$\mathcal{A}$bove: *This repair job entailed replacing both the spokes and the weavers, which is obviously a bit more involved than simply replacing broken weavers.*

maintain its antique value, an authentic Colonial chair that's missing its seat should probably be rewoven with natural rush (rather than fiber rush), because that's what was used on the original chair.

One of the best ways to learn about good and bad wicker and what is easy to repair or too costly or impossible to repair is to get out and look at what's available. Examine each piece closely and pretty soon you'll come to recognize quality. You'll also find your bargaining power increases as you demonstrate that you know what to look for when you shop. Sometimes dealers don't know how easy certain repairs are to make, so you may be able to negotiate to your advantage on damaged wicker.

To find crafters who repair old wicker and cane, check the Yellow Pages under "Antiques—Repairing and Restoration," "Furniture—Repairing and Refinishing," and "Caning." Or you can sometimes find them by word of mouth, if you ask around at antique shops and auctions. Prices vary widely, depending on the job, but are rarely cheap, so you may want to get some ballpark estimates over the phone before commiting to one. Some wicker restorers have a minimum fee of $100 (£60), for instance; others may give you a discount if they don't have to pick up and deliver the piece.

Prices on chair repair are a little more straightforward. Re-doing hand caned seats is usually charged by the hole, with prices ranging from 80 cents to $1.50 a hole (50 pence to £1); prewoven cane and fiber rush are charged by the inch, measuring across the chair, at anywhere from $2.25 to $3.00 (£1 to £2). Natural rush repair will run $5.00 (£3) per inch.

Your basic criteria for judging wicker involves three things: the framework, the woven material, and the finish. This holds true for both old and new wicker, but is especially important with old pieces, which tend to be less than perfect. The woven material is especially vulnerable, as time has often taken its toll through neglect and extreme conditions. Although it's beyond the scope of this book to detail the variety of possible repairs, you need to have some idea of best and worst case scenarios: jobs that are a piece of cake to accomplish versus those you'd be better off avoiding. The following sections will get you started, but in order to gain absolute confidence in your judgment, you'll probably need to do some additional research. Get out and look at all the wicker you can, talk to dealers and repair people, and above all, pay close attention to details. Examine each piece you come across thoroughly and you'll find yourself learning without even consciously trying to do so.

*B*elow: *Replacing a cane seat requires patience, foresight, and attention to detail.*

© J.P. Tesson/H. Armstrong Roberts

© Lynn Karlin/Courtesy Trenton Avenue Antique Center, Maine

QUICK FIXES

Just because something's damaged doesn't necessarily mean you should pass it by. The following problems are easy (and relatively inexpensive) to repair:

- *Missing wrapping.* If the cane or fiber rush wrapping around a leg or arm of an old chair is loose or missing, it's a breeze to replace.

- *Sagging cane seat.* If the seat is unbroken, but seems stretched out, this can often be rectified by simply wetting the underside of the cane and letting it dry. You may have to repeat this procedure several times, but eventually the seat should shrink back up to tautness.

- *Braid damaged in spots.* Broken braid can be rewoven without too much trouble. (If it's heavily damaged or missing, the braid may need to be replaced. This is fairly easy to accomplish, but more time consuming.)

- *Loose scrollwork.* Scrollwork, you recall, consists of loops or curlicues and is commonly found on the backs or arms of Victorian pieces. As long as it's intact, scrollwork is easy to fix. If it's broken or missing, however, repairing scrollwork is more difficult, though still perfectly possible.

- *Weavers broken or missing in spots.* The weavers are the horizontal reeds that go over and under the spokes, or vertical reeds. As long as the piece was handwoven and the damage is minimal, this is an easy job, even on serpentine areas.

Left: *Auctions and estate sales are excellent sources of slightly damaged old wicker; sometimes, it can even be had for bargain prices. As long as the reed isn't broken, a sagging cane seat (above) is easy to fix. Simply wet the underside of the cane and let the seat dry.*

- *Spokes broken or missing in spots.* Spokes are the vertical reeds used as the basis for weaving, and as long as they aren't on serpentine areas (which is a more involved project, though not impossible), they shouldn't be too much trouble to repair. Just make sure the spokes have wire centers if they're made of fiber rush; if they don't, forget it—the piece is inferior and not worth bothering with.

- *Broken pairing weave.* Pairing weave describes two reeds that are twisted horizontally on Bar Harbor-style pieces to help hold the spokes in place as well as to add strength. Since pairing weave is found on open weave pieces, it's easy to reach and fix.

How Old Is It?

To qualify as a bona fide antique, furniture must be more than one hundred years old. Antiques are judged by authenticity and condition, as well as by scarcity; the rarer a piece is, the more expensive it will be. However, there are plenty of beautiful wicker pieces that aren't old enough to be real antiques, but are valuable and collectible none the less. Wicker

With a little practice, you'll soon recognize which repairs are worth making. Right: This hourglass table looks pretty bad, but aside from needing a new top, it is in excellent condition. Opposite page: Antique wicker and rustic chairs are available in a variety of styles.

© Daniella Jo Nilva

made as late as the 1930s can still be highly desirable, but the main thing is to be aware of exactly what you're getting.

Volumes have been written on how to date and price old wicker furniture, and it's beyond the scope of this book to go into explicit detail. Price is determined by age, condition, and appraisal value, so the best way to learn about market values is to shop around. In general, through the years the styles have gotten simpler (though not necessarily cheaper). The following chart offers some general guidelines for placing pieces in their broad historical contexts.

TIMETABLE OF WICKER STYLES

1850s   French Rococo-style furniture, featuring ornate designs and curved lines, started to gain popularity in America. This early furniture was often made of bentwood that was then covered with rattan. (British designs of the same period were extremely simple, consisting mostly of variations on the basket chair.)

1876

Courtesy Dover Publications, Inc.

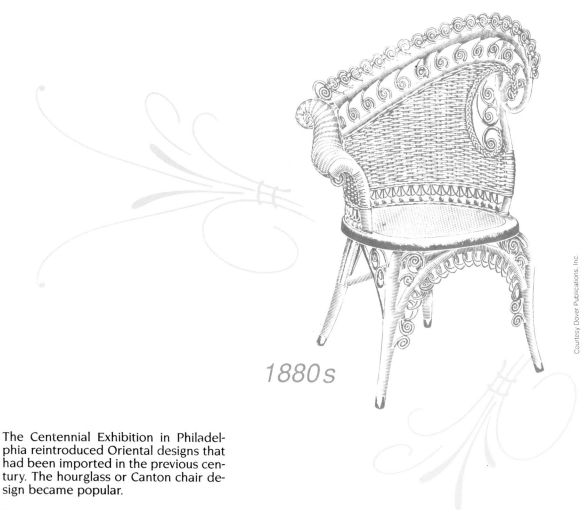

1880s

Courtesy Dover Publications, Inc.

1876   The Centennial Exhibition in Philadel-
        phia reintroduced Oriental designs that
        had been imported in the previous cen-
        tury. The hourglass or Canton chair de-
        sign became popular.

1880s   Wicker began to be manufactured in
        the United States on a large scale. Com-
        binations of materials and styles in-
        cluded Rococo, Classical, Gothic, and
        many variations. The furniture might be
        left natural or lightly stained, and was
        usually painted for indoor use. (NOTE:
        Natural Victorian wicker is worth twice
        as much as its painted equivalent.)

1900s   Designs became more sedate, less curvy, as decorating tastes changed. Mission, straight-line furniture was in vogue, and the hourglass chair returned, along with complete sets of furniture made in that shape. Open weave Bar Harbor pieces appeared.

1904   Fiber rush was invented in this year but didn't really catch on until 1920. Thus, anything made of this synthetic material is not authentically Victorian.

1917   The Lloyd loom was invented, enabling fiber rush to be woven into a "cloth" that was then attached to the frame by hand. Cape Cod style, closely woven wicker, became less expensive.

1920s   Art Deco furniture appeared, and wicker manufacturers adapted their designs to fit the new style. Upholstered wicker with removable cushions were popular. Many Art Deco wicker pieces featured a small diamond design in a contrasting color on the back.

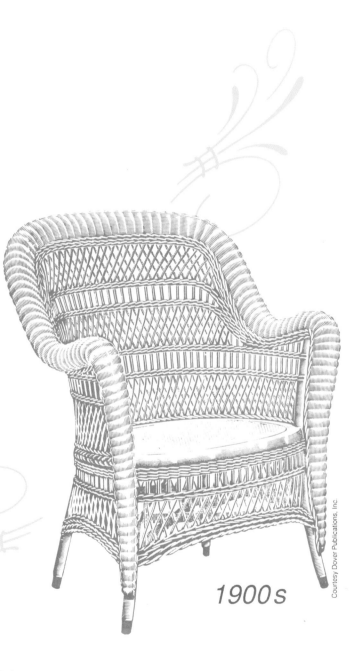

1900s

Courtesy Dover Publications, Inc.

Where to Buy Old Wicker

Many of the sources for purchasing old wicker can be found in your newspaper, including notices of auctions, estate sales, flea markets, and garage sales, as well as special classified listings. Antique shops, listed in the Yellow Pages, tend to be more expensive, but shouldn't be overlooked, especially if you're having trouble finding some specific piece you've fallen in love with.

Auctions: As a rule, at an auction you'll pay two-thirds of what you would in an antique shop for the same piece, so this is where educated consumers usually congregate. But although you can get a better price than you might elsewhere, the trick is to know what you're willing to pay, then stick to it.

If possible, get a catalog or description of the sale beforehand. Besides providing information on the pieces for sale, it should also explain conditions: arrangements for payment, how soon you must remove purchases, and responsibilities of the buyer and auctioneer.

Attend the preview (usually held the day before the sale) and check out the pieces you might be interested in. Inspect furniture closely, turning it over to check construction techniques and materials. If you notice damage that's not irreparable, figure the cost of repairs

© Lynn Karlin/Courtesy Trenton Avenue Antique Center, Maine

This antique chair (above) features a scrollwork back with a heart motif, a design much beloved by the Victorians.

© James R. Levin/FPG International

into your bid. (For example, if you wanted to pay no more than $200 |£120| and figure the repairs at $50 |£30|, your top bid should be $150 |£90|.)

Carefully examine anything you're even remotely interested in, because you should *never* bid on a piece you haven't checked out up close. You won't see flaws or missing pieces from a distance, and you can't bid realistically if you don't know about specific shortcomings.

On the day of the auction, be prepared to spend hours, or even the entire day there, if there's something you want to bid on. During the actual bidding, keep your cool. Wear your best poker face, since the auctioneer may try and manipulate the bidding to take advantage of your eagerness if you're too obviously excited about a piece. Also, be sure you understand exactly what you're bidding on. Is it the sofa and the armchair, or just the sofa? Should you win, write down the exact amount of your bid and hold on to your bidding number. Be sure and get a receipt.

Old-fashioned wicker seating adds character to a
modern deck (left).

LET THE BUYER BEWARE

Some things are better left alone—they're hopeless. The following list indicates serious flaws that, if encountered, should automatically disqualify a piece.

- A *rotten or damaged framework*. Always turn a piece over and inspect the frame. Although sometimes missing parts can be replaced, if the frame is broken or cracked or if the wood itself is rotten, the piece is not worth bothering with.

- *Brittle reed or fiber rush that snaps like uncooked spaghetti when bent*. The piece was probably exposed to temperature and climatic extremes; there is no way to revive wicker that's this far gone.

- *Broken fiber rush spokes without wire centers on the back of a chair or sofa*. As explained above, this indicates inferior quality materials—all the spokes will eventually need to be replaced.

- *Broken spokes on a loom-woven piece*. Since replacement spokes must be forced into place through many tight rows of weavers, this problem can be more trouble than it's worth to fix.

- *Badly weathered fiber rush*. If the surface of a fiber rush piece is in bad condition—the paint is cracked or flaking, for instance—it's impossible to restore.

- A *"fuzzy" surface*. Look closely to make sure the paint or varnish looks smooth. If it's fuzzy, the finish has been improperly sanded and sprayed.

- *Excess paint globbed into the weave*. If all the holes in the weave are obliterated by paint, it's a Herculean labor to correct; each one must be reopened by pushing an ice pick through the weave.

- *Uncomfortable*. This is important enough to bear repeating: If you intend to use the piece to sit on, make sure you like the way it feels.

Opposite page: *Old wicker sometimes turns up at flea markets, but it's not always a bargain. Before making a purchase shop around a bit and inspect the piece carefully.*

Estate Sales: Estate sales are held when someone dies and the heirs don't want the property, or can't decide how to divide it equally, as well as sometimes in cases of divorce or relocation. Because a lot of perfectly good wicker was banished to the attic decades ago, it often shows up at estate sales. You can sometimes find matched sets at reasonable prices.

Some collectors prefer estate sales because they're guaranteed that the merchandise hasn't been offered for sale before, whereas auctions sometimes recycle the same items show after show. An estate sale has legal status and a real one is registered with the Probate Court.

Estate sales can be conducted as an auction or as a tag sale, and are held either at the auctioneer's site or at the seller's home. Newspaper notices of these sales sometimes include a bill of goods; in the case of auctions, you'll need to attend the preview, usually held the day before.

In the case of a tag sale, an appraiser comes to the seller's home and labels each item with a price. Then, on the day of the sale small groups of people are allowed into the house, usually ten at a time, to make their purchases. The early birds obviously get the best selection, but latecomers may be able to dicker with the appraiser about leftovers.

Flea Markets and Garage Sales: Your chances of finding quality wicker aren't quite as good here as at estate sales and auctions, but if you are lucky enough to find some, then these pieces may be priced well below market value. This is especially true at garage sales, where people are usually more interested simply in unloading household clutter than in making

money from it, and may be unaware of what they really have.

I recently heard of an extreme example of this. One morning a friend of mine saw an entire wicker porch set on her eighty-year-old neighbor's curb, waiting to be taken away as trash. Although the furniture dated back to the 1920s and was in excellent condition, the

© Lynn Karlin

© D.G. Arnold

T̲his antique rocker (above) has the serpentine line
characteristic of many Victorian pieces. You'll probably pay top
dollar for wicker furniture at an antique store (opposite page),
but go ahead and browse. Dealers can teach you a lot about what
to look for in old wicker, and may prove invaluable in tracking
down something specific.

neighbor said she "didn't want to be bothered
with trying to sell the old junk," and just wanted
it out of her house! Obviously she had no idea
it was worth more than a thousand dollars.

Classified Listings: These are good because
they're specific, so you can zero in on what
you're looking for without leaving home. Many
cities have special newspapers devoted entirely to classifieds; arranged alphabetically or
indexed by category, these listings often prove
happy hunting grounds for collectors.

Another advantage to classifieds is that you
can screen things over the phone—if you're
looking for natural wicker and when you call
about a piece you discover it's been painted,
you'll save yourself a trip. Develop a list of
questions, such as how old the piece is, who
manufacturered it, whether or not it's ever
been repaired, etc. Find out as much as you
can before going to see a piece.

If you decide to go and look at something,
remember that you're under no obligation to
buy. Occasionally people may try and use high-
pressure techniques on you, or you may actually feel guilty for wasting their time if you find
you aren't interested. But never buy anything
you don't really want or are unsure about,
because you're bound to regret it later.

Antique Shops: These are great places to
learn about old wicker styles as well as about

© Lynn Karlin/Courtesy Trenton Avenue Antique Center, Maine

current market values. Though you'll rarely find a bargain, dealers can sometimes provide valuable assistance in tracking down hard-to-find pieces, and the extra money may be a fair trade-off for the aggravation you'll avoid. In any case, knowledgeable dealers can be worth their weight in gold when it comes to advice on what to look for in wicker furniture.

Check the Yellow Pages and phone various stores to see who has a good selection of wicker; you may also be able to gauge a dealer's helpfulness over the phone. (Why deal with someone crotchety if you can avoid it?)

R*ight: Modern reproductions of old-style wicker generally cost much less than the originals, plus they are sold in matched sets, which antiques rarely are.*

B*UYING* N*EW* W*ICKER*

When you buy quality wicker, cane, willow, and rattan furniture, you're guaranteed years of enjoyment. Contemporary wicker is available in a variety of styles, represented by innumerable pieces and room groupings, so you're bound to find something just right for your existing decor or to suit your personality.

For instance, if you like the look of old wicker but get impatient with the search, or don't care to bother with repairs, check out what manufacturers are offering in the way of reproductions. Many companies sell designs inspired by antique wicker created in the past, while others reproduce old designs verbatim. For instance, Bielecky Brothers now reissues some authentic reproductions that were popular from the 1920s through the 1940s in their "Vintage Collection." Other companies sell furniture groupings that feature the Art Deco triangles that were popular in the 1920s, but today have a certain Southwestern flavor.

Though many experts tout the superior craftsmanship of antiques, high-quality wicker that's being manufactured today is every bit as good as the old stuff. The furniture sold by Western companies tends to be better than what's imported from the East, even though most companies are forced to have at least some of their work done overseas. Since the early 1980s, foreign governments have restricted the export of rattan poles. Thus the frame and weaving are usually completed abroad, then shipped here for finishing and upholstering.

Courtesy Wickerware Inc.

The main difference with the wicker imported from the East is the finish. Western companies use a glossy enamel that's as shiny as a new car, and extremely durable. The paints available in the Third World countries where most wicker is produced just can't match these products. Nor do they have the technology to do a state-of-the-art job. For instance, Ficks Reed, a leading American manufacturer, uses a finishing process that involves seven to ten different procedures—toning, sealing, glazing, rubbing, padding, brushing, etc.—and fourteen separate sandings.

Another drawback on imported furniture is the cushions—the stuffing and fabrics are inferior to those available here. For instance, fabric designs may be dated, and cottons won't be protected, i.e., Scotchgarded. Also, because imported cushions must be soaked in formaldehyde to meet stringent Customs standards,

© M. Eckert/FPG International

they stink. Thus, most Western manufacturers produce their cushions at home.

With better manufacturers, you're not always restricted to the cushions that come with the piece—some will provide swatches of available fabrics so you can choose your favorite. Occasionally a manufacturer will even cover the cushions with a fabric you provide.

Sometimes the craftsmanship on imported pieces is lacking as well. The drawers may not be faced or may not pull smoothly. But if you are willing to live with such flaws (or fix them yourself—sticky drawers can be sanded and waxed, for instance), you may be able to get a discount. Point out obvious defects to the seller, and complain that you shouldn't have to pay for them. You'd be surprised how well this can work, since sellers are usually well aware of these defects themselves, and count on customers to overlook them.

W*icker has a universal quality that allows it to cohabitate gracefully with traditional furnishings* (left).

Wicker Checklist

As with old wicker, the quality of new wicker varies widely, so you need to be alert. The same three criteria of framework, woven material, and finish serve for evaluation here, as does the basic "shake" test. (Bearing down slightly, grasp the piece with both hands and shake it. It should feel solid and shouldn't wiggle much.) The following list outlines some of the main things to watch for.

- Sturdy construction. The frame should be secured with glue, nails, or screws, and fit closely, without shake.

- Joints should have genuine cane bindings for strength. Check to make sure the bindings aren't plastic, which is an indication of inferior quality.

- Fungus or mildew marks. New, natural wicker should be free of marks that indicate fungus or mildew—an overall gray color, with a dull look.

- Beware of fuzz. Look closely to make sure the paint or varnish looks smooth. If it's fuzzy, the finish has been improperly sanded and sprayed.

- On unfinished wicker, make sure the surface is smooth, without splinters.

- On Cape Cod wicker, old or new, look closely at the weave. Each row should be straight and tight, without gaps.

- Tabletop moldings should be set flush with the top. Mitered corners indicate superior construction, and again, the whole piece should be balanced and stable, without wobbles.

- Check under cushions. If it's a strap support design, the straps should be attached to a separate seat frame, not directly to the rattan or bamboo.

- Rattan furniture should be free of discoloration and other physical defects. Growth nodes should be spaced twelve to eighteen inches (thirty to forty-six centimeters) apart and be uniform in size—indications of a mature plant.

- Quality rattan will have a smoother, less knobby look than lower quality pieces. It will probably be sturdier as well.

Right: *In extreme cases of dried out wicker, the garden hose may actually be helpful, but usually a vacuuming followed by a once over with a damp rag is enough to maintain wicker.*

© Christopher Bain

CARE AND MAINTENANCE OF
WICKER, CANE, AND WILLOW

If well cared for, this furniture will last for generations. It is delicate, yet durable, and has the advantage of never needing to be waxed or polished. An occasional once over with a damp cloth or vacuum will keep it looking great, and it's easy to touch up if the finish gets nicked.

Cleaning Wicker

They used to think you should hose down wicker furniture outside, but now general opinion has it that you should vacuum it with the brush attachment, then wipe it with a cloth dipped in warm water and a mild household cleanser. ("Mild" means anything that's safe to use on woodwork, and is less likely to harm fragile fibers and glue joints.) But since wicker is more pliable when damp, it should definitely be wiped with a wet cloth periodically to keep it supple. Don't overwater, however, as this may cause mildew to appear.

Both painted and natural wicker can be maintained as described above; in extreme cases, however, you may actually need to use the hose on your wicker. If a chair or sofa makes small popping noises, it's too dry and should be soaked or dampened. If wicker is allowed to dry out completely, it will become brittle and break; water feeds the reeds, insuring greater flexibility and a longer life.

At the other extreme, if wicker stays damp for too long, it's liable to mildew. If you should have the misfortune to encounter mildew on your wicker furniture, have the cushions professionally cleaned, and wash the piece with a disinfectant cleaner or a mixture of ¼ cup bleach to a quart of water. (Since this will lighten the colors, be sure to wash the whole thing.) Air the cushions frequently in direct sunlight to prevent mold and mildew from redeveloping.

On antique wicker, use an old toothbrush to scrub accumulated grime out of the crevices in the weave; if you maintain new wicker regularly, you shouldn't have to resort to this. If the piece is extremely dirty and the toothbrush technique seems overly tedious, you can use an air compressor and a blow gun to blast grime out of the crevices. Or you can try using a solution of well-diluted household bleach if the finish doesn't seem to be coming clean. (Again, you'll have to scrub the entire piece to maintain a uniform color.)

To restore lustre to a dull finish that's been lacquered, shellacked, or varnished, use a soft cloth and rub lemon oil or furniture polish over the piece. Minor scratches can be erased with wax-based compounds.

Cane seats should also be wiped with a damp cloth periodically. Once dry, they can be treated with an oil-based product such as linseed or lemon oil to help maintain suppleness.

Bent willow furniture is practically maintenance-free; it can be dusted like any other wooden furniture, and needs just a very occasional oiling to bring out the beautiful deep tones of the wood. If used indoors, willow furniture needs to be treated with linseed oil about once a year. Simply take the piece outdoors and brush on the linseed oil, then allow it to dry outdoors for a day or two. If it's used outdoors, it needs a linseed-oil treatment two or three times a year.

Bent willow furniture (above) *is easy to care for, as it requires only dusting and an occasional oiling to bring out the beauty of the wood.*

Wicker No-Nos

Wicker as a rule is very strong and durable. But if it's exposed to extreme conditions, an alternate Old Norse derivation of the word wicker, *veikr*, meaning "weak," may begin to apply. The following circumstances should be avoided at all costs:

- Don't place wicker or cane seats near radiators or heat vents; this will weaken cane bindings and dry out the reed.

- Avoid direct sunlight—it dries out the fibers and makes them prone to splitting, as well as bleaching the finish.

- Avoid high humidity, especially if the furniture has cushions, because mildew may develop.

- Don't use unfinished wicker outdoors unless it's been lacquered or varnished.

- Never leave wicker furniture outdoors in winter if you live in a temperate climate.

- Never hose down fiber rush furniture—it will fall apart!

I*deally, wicker used outdoors should be placed in at least partial shade (below), since direct sunlight will dry it out and make it age prematurely.*

© Steven Brooke

 Refinishing Wicker

Sometimes you'll come across old wicker that's structurally sound, but the finish leaves a lot to be desired. Although in some cases it's hopeless—fiber rush that's badly weathered, for instance, or paint that's globbed thickly into all the holes in the weave—other times it's a fairly simple matter to restore a piece to its former glory with a little fresh paint.

There is some controversy about whether or not wicker can be stripped. The general consensus is that it's not a good idea; the few who do suggest the possibility admit that it's an iffy

© Gerard Fritz/FPG International

job, and unanimously agree that it should be left to professionals. If you decide to risk it, be forewarned that the strong chemicals used in stripping tend to weaken the reed, and may cause damage that won't show up until after the piece is repainted or refinished. Fiber rush, on the other hand, should never be stripped, because the scrubbing required to remove the old paint or varnish will tear up the surface irrevocably.

Touch-Ups

Touch-ups are easy, if the problem is minor— just a little flaking paint here and there. The hardest part of the whole project is probably matching the paint color; this is simplified if you happen to have some leftover paint of the right color, otherwise, you'll have to improvise. Although you can use spray paint in a can, the chances of getting an exact color match are pretty slim. Artists' acrylics are probably your best bet, since they are sold in small tubes in a variety of colors, so you can experiment with mixing paints. Acrylics can be used over latex or oil-based paints, and dry quickly. (If you have too much trouble getting a color to match, take a paint chip from your wicker with you to the paint store and get them to help you match the paint colors.)

To begin, scrub off loose paint with a wire brush and lots of water, then allow the piece to dry thoroughly. Once dry, seal with a primer and then apply a few light coats of paint, being sure to let each coat dry completely before painting over it. (A cotton swab works well for touching up little nicks.)

Touching up stain can also be tricky, as you get into color matching again. If the stain you purchase isn't exactly the right color, you may have to experiment with mixing artists' acrylics. Yellow ochre, burnt sienna, raw sienna, burnt umber, Indian red, black, and white are good candidates to try. Start light and work darker, as you can always make a color darker but it's very hard to lighten a shade. Try colors in an out-of-sight or inconspicuous area until you're sure you've got a match.

Peeling or flaking paint on cane chairs (left) can be handled like any other refinishing job.

Dull, worn spots on clear, finished wicker can be touched up with lacquer. First sand the problem spots lightly, then use a small paintbrush or cotton swab to daub on the clear finish. Be sparing with the lacquer to avoid clogging the weave.

Painting or Refinishing an Entire Piece

If too many areas need touch-ups, you may be better off redoing the entire piece. (This also applies when there've been some repairs, and touching them up makes them stand out rather than blend in.)

It's fairly simple to refinish a natural wicker piece. First rub it with mineral spirits to dull the finish, then brush or spray on a wood stain or varnish in whatever shade you prefer. Once the first coat is dry, follow with additional coats if necessary, then finish with a coat of polyurethane to protect the surface.

For painting wicker, spray paints work best because they'll deposit an adequate coat on the outer surfaces while giving minimum coverage to the inner weave, where it's least needed. Brushing tends to spread the finish too thinly on the outer surfaces while glomming it up in the weave, though it can produce satisfactory results if you're careful. For the most profes-sional-looking paint job, however, rent an air compressor and spray gun; it will automatically provide the fine, light mist you need to do a good job of spray painting. As an extra precaution, strain paints and varnishes before using.

Thin coats dry faster and look better, plus they're more durable and less likely to chip. Enamel paint is most commonly used; it will cover in one coat if the piece is well primed, and this will reduce runs and drips. High-gloss exterior enamel works well, but be sure to use only the best paints and varnishes—cheap stuff is no bargain!

*P*ainted wicker (right) *adds pizazz to any room; the color you choose can complement your decor. Here, green is the perfect color for this country-style room.*

© Jeff McNamara

© Jeff McNamara

UNFINISHED WICKER

Unfinished wicker should be vacuumed and wiped periodically, as described above. It must be lacquered or varnished if you intend to use it outdoors, but much of its natural look can be preserved if you use a clear, penetrating, waterproofing sealer. This will darken the fibers somewhat, but it won't look shiny. To see how it will look, dampen a small portion of the unfinished wicker with water. The sealer will look about the same, once applied.

Unfinished wicker can also be dyed, giving it a subtle look. Dyed color is more durable than paint because it actually penetrates the fibers rather than just coating the surface; thus, dye will never peel or flake. For an idea of how dyed wicker looks, check out colored baskets at a craft store or gift shop. Instructions on dyeing wicker can be found in Chapter Three, page 121.

U*nfinished wicker* (opposite page) *can be used as is for an organic, earthy look. A clear, waterproofing sealer will help protect unfinished furniture without interfering with the natural beauty of the wood* (right).

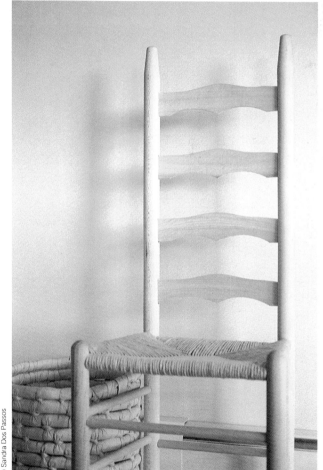

© Sandra Dos Passos

Eternal Wicker

If you buy quality pieces and take good care of them, wicker, cane, and willow furniture will last for generations. Although purchasing furniture can be intimidating, since it's an investment you'll live with for years, you can protect yourself by shopping around. The best way to become a savvy shopper is to browse and ask lots of questions. Inspect as many pieces as you can, wherever you encounter them, whether you're actually interested in buying a particular piece or not. With a little practice, you'll find yourself automatically checking frames and weaves and finishes; your evaluation of craftsmanship will become second nature. So enjoy the thrill of the chase, and don't settle for anything you're not 100 percent happy with. This furniture may be around longer than you are; let it be a legacy you're proud to leave behind.

© Lynn Karlin/Courtesy Trenton Avenue Antique Center, Maine

An antique rocker (left) adds character and charm to any room in the house. Right: The right combination of table and chair can help create a comfortable, relaxed atmosphere, indoors or out.

© Lynn Karlin/Courtesy Trenton Avenue Antique Center, Maine

© Ralph Bogertman

© Ralph Bogertman

© Ralph Bogertman

© Ralph Bogertman

Chapter Three
WORKING WITH WICKER, CANE, AND WILLOW

This chapter contains seven step-by-step projects that use wicker, cane, or willow. They range from fairly simple—painting and dying wicker—to more complex and involved—recaning a chair and making your own twig plant stand take a little more time and patience, yet the outcome is well worth it. Included with each project is a list of the materials needed, as well as photographs of the project in progress.

When undertaking a repair project, remember that it may be necessary to order some of the needed materials—such as lengths of wicker or cane—ahead of time. You can phone or visit your local craft shop to see if they have it in stock, or phone the manufacturer directly.

When ordering wicker, you should always include a sample of the wicker that needs repairing, since it comes in a variety of standard gauges. When ordering cane, it is best to bring a sample of the object you are repairing along with you to the store (or send it if you are ordering by mail), since cane comes in six standard widths.

Before beginning any project, it is recommended that you carefully read through the directions first. This way, you will know if anything needs to be prepared ahead of time. For instance, both wicker and cane need to be soaked in water for ten minutes before they are pliant enough to work with.

Wicker Repair

Materials needed:
lengths of wicker
garden shears or sharp knife
warm water
container for soaking wicker

1 Clean out all of the broken or bent weavers (horizontal wicker), leaving the spokes (verticle supports) intact. Stagger the edges of the remaining weavers by cutting some long, others short, to resemble a zigzag rather than a comb. This will provide a better weaving base.

2 Soak a few lengths of new wicker in warm water for ten minutes. The wicker will then be pliable and easy to work with, but don't let it soak too long, or it will get fibrous and weak.

3 Carefully study the overall pattern of the existing weave. You must follow the over-under pattern exactly to ensure an even repair.

4 Starting at the top left-hand corner, secure the end of a length of wicker by placing it under the existing wicker; leave a couple of inches at that end to ensure that the wicker stays firmly in place. Gently, but firmly, pass the longer length of remaining wicker over and under the existing spokes. This over-under rhythm should take you to the edge of the right side. Guide the wicker under the existing weave; once firm, cut near the end.

5 Repeat this process until the repair area has been fully covered.

6 Once the repair is completely dry, paint it to match the existing color.

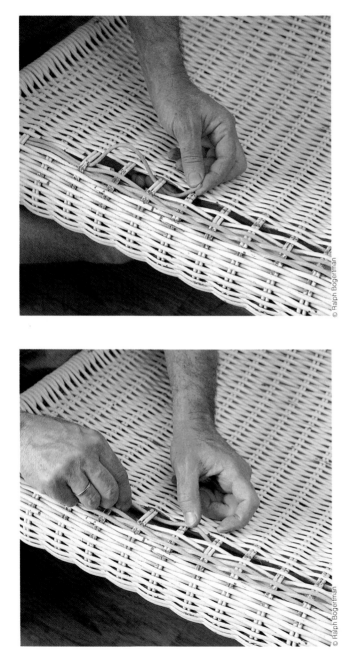

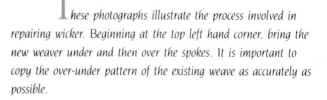

These photographs illustrate the process involved in repairing wicker. Beginning at the top left hand corner, bring the new weaver under and then over the spokes. It is important to copy the over-under pattern of the existing weave as accurately as possible.

© Ralph Bogertman

Caning A Chair

Materials needed:

a sharp penknife
wooden pegs (or golf tees)
cane (sized to match chair)
binder cane

Cane comes from the tough outer layer of rattan, which is machine-cut into strips. Available in six standard widths, the widest being binder and decreasing to common, medium, fine, finefine, and superfine. Since there are so many possible gauges of cane, the best way to replace a seat is to bring along (or send, if mail-ordering) a sample of the original. If no portions of the original remain, measure the diameter of the holes around the rim, or better yet, trace one or two onto a piece of paper, and take or mail that.

Note that the cane has a top and a bottom side; the top has a sheen. Always weave with the cane flat, top side up. Avoid bending or twisting cane to ensure durability.

The pegs are used to hold down the loose ends of the cane until they are tied, as well as to keep woven strands of cane taut. Golf tees work well, or you can make your own pegs by cutting dowels into 3-inch (8-centimeter)

lengths, and then sharpening one end with a pencil sharpener.

1 Once you have cleared a work space and assembled your materials, study any existing caning to see how the pattern and binding were executed. All the old weaving must be removed before you begin, so take a good look. Then use the knife to cut around the edge of the chair seat, removing the center. Next, cut the cane out of the holes. All holes must be clear, if some have pegs in them, use a 2-inch (5-centimeter) nail and a hammer to knock these out. (If these pegs have been glued in place, you may need to drill them.)

2 Put a few strands of cane in warm water to soak for ten minutes. The cane needs to be pliable for you to work with it, so keep three strands soaking ahead as you begin to weave.

3 Find the center hole on the front and back side of the chair. Insert cane down through the center hole in the back of the chair and let it extend 4 or 5 inches (10 or 12 centimeters). Secure it with a peg. Take the remaining length of cane and pass it through the front center hole and pull it taut; again, place a peg to hold the tension. Bring the cane up through the next hole on the left of the center hole in the front of the chair, and then back to the left-of-center hole at the rear. Keep this pattern going until all the rear holes are filled, being careful to keep all woven strands parallel. (Since the woven strands must be parallel, on round seats you may find it necessary to skip a hole to maintain a parallel configuration.) Repeat the weaving pattern to finish the right half.

4 Begin this step by starting at the hole next to the corner hole of the side rail at the rear. The cane should be carried across the seat and always over the existing woven pattern. It is important to keep the corner holes free because you will use them when finishing off the caning process. You may have to use the corner holes of the seat if the seat is curved. If your seat is round, begin on the side at the center point and develop the parallel pattern as you did in step 3. Start at the center hole and work to the left, filling in the back, and then repeat that process from the next center hole, filling in to the right front of the seat.

5 This process is the same as step 3. You use the same holes as you did in step 3, but keep this strand to the right of the first strand.

In this photograph (right), the recaning process has just begun. Remember to bring the cane from the back of the chair to the front, pulling it taut after each step, and inserting a peg to hold the tension; this will keep it from sagging.

© Ralph Bogertman

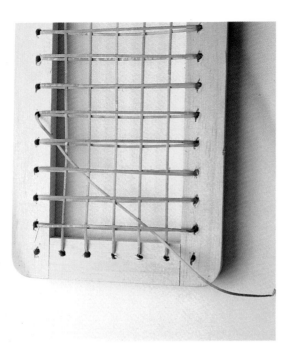

© Ralph Bogerman

T*his photograph* (above) *portrays the second diagonal strand woven, described in step 8. It begins at the left back and goes to the right front.*

6 This is the first actual weaving step, and it is critical in the development of the basic pattern. This step is parallel to step 4, and uses the same holes. Begin on the left side in the rear left hole, and take the cane in front of step 4, passing it under step 3 and over step 5.

7 This strand of cane is the first to run on a diagonal. It begins at the right front and goes to the rear left. Remember, cane will run from front to rear. This strand goes under steps 3 and 5, and over steps 4 and 6.

8 This is the second diagonal strand you'll weave; it is done in the opposite pattern of step 7. The cane will go over steps 3 and 5, and under steps 4, 6, and 7.

9 Tie off the loose ends on the underside of the chair. When secure, cut the ends back to about an inch (2.5 centimeters).

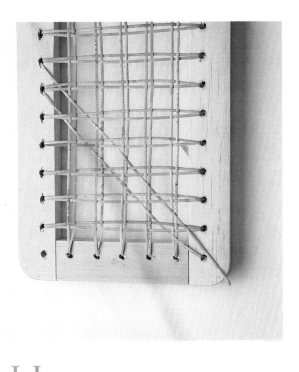

Here, the seat is on its way to being recaned; the caning pattern is clearly emerging.

10 Finish the top edge of cane seats with a special strip of cane called a binder. If your seat is square, measure four equal lengths, allowing about five inches (13 centimeters) extra. If your seat is round, measure one length of binder, allowing the same 5 inches (13 centimeters).

11 Lay the binder over the row of holes on one side of the chair. Insert binder end into the last hole. Peg to secure. You may cut the peg off flush with the top of the chair seat. To bind the binder, take a strand of the cane you were using to cane the chair, and insert the strand from the underside of the seat up and over, and pass through the same hole to underside. Advance around the chair following this process, keeping the strand as taut as possible. When you reach the end, lap the first end over the second end and tie them down.

Courtesy Palecek

PAINTING PROCEDURE

1 Clean the piece thoroughly. Vacuum and wipe with a damp cloth, then allow the surface to dry thoroughly.

2 Sand the rough spots. With very fine sandpaper, work over areas of chipped or flaking paint, or spots where dust particles were trapped in the paint. On unfinished wicker, sand off splinters or places where the reed has split. Some people use a liquid sanding preparation instead of sanding. These products, sold in paint or hardware stores, remove dirt, grease, and oils, and soften the surface of the old paint to help it bond with the new.

3 Prepare the area. Spray-painting should be done outdoors on a dry, windless day. Spread a drop cloth on the ground and hang another one from a clothesline as a backdrop. This will help prevent billows of toxic paint mist from blowing around. Wear a mask or respirator to avoid breathing paint vapors.

4 Prime the piece. Primer is the secret of a professional-looking paint job—especially if you plan to use a different color than is currently on there, or if the piece is unfinished. It will seal the surface and provide a good base for the paint to adhere to. Use a spray primer (a compressed air gun, again, gives the best results), and allow for several light coats if you're trying to cover a color.

5 Paint the piece. Control is the key here, because less is definitely more when it comes to spray paint. With a gentle back-and-forth motion, let a light mist of paint fall evenly across the piece. Build up coverage gradually—don't try to do it all at once. Spray until the piece looks wet, but not runny; do another coat rather than trying to cover too much. You want to avoid drips at all costs—should you make a mistake, you'll have to let it dry, sand it down, and start over. Always allow paint to dry thoroughly before adding another coat.

DYEING WORDS

Small things like baskets can be immersed in the bathtub; larger pieces will need to be sponged. But don't use aluminum, copper, galvanized pans, or anything you use to prepare food for dyeing, as the chemicals are contaminating. Avoid working in food-preparation areas for the same reason. Plastic buckets are probably best, and wear rubber gloves unless you want to walk around with dyed hands for three days afterward.

- To dye wicker in the bathtub, you'll need half a bottle (4 oz.) or one package of dye for every three gallons of water.

- To dye wicker using the sponge-on method, use one bottle of dye to ½ cup hot water.

For darker, more intense colors, use more dye; for pastels, use less. Just remember that unlike fabric, dyed wicker is approximately the same color wet as dry, so what you see is what you get.

1   Prepare the piece. Wicker will take dye better if it has a dull surface. If it feels too smooth, sand it lightly.

2   Prepare the area. If immersing a piece in the bathtub, remove shower curtains and throw rugs—anything you'd care about if it accidentally got splattered with dye. If using the sponge-on method, spread a large plastic drop cloth on the floor.

3   Mix up the dye. Whether you're immersing or using the sponge-on method, it's imperative that the dye be thoroughly dissolved. If it isn't, you'll get small dots of intense color where clumps of undissolved powder land. Use a small bottle to mix up powdered dye with hot water; strain mixture through a cheesecloth as an extra precaution. Never pour dye directly on wicker, as this will create a blotchy color.

4 Dye the piece. When immersing an object, keep it moving constantly to avoid streaking. Leave it in the dye bath for about fifteen to twenty minutes, or until it reaches the desired shade. When using the sponge-on method, use a large sponge to wipe the color onto the wicker, continuing until it's the color you want. Let the dye set for ten minutes before rinsing.

5 Rinse with cold water. Whichever method you use, do not neglect this step! Excess dye will rub off on fabric, so rinse the piece well—by immersion or with the sponge, with plenty of clean water. This will also help set the dye and work it into the crevices.

© Jeff McNamara

VINE BASKET

Materials needed:
heavy-duty garden clippers
vines

If you like, you can gather your own vines; take a walk through the woods and look for grapevines and wisteria, or any other vines that suit your fancy. Look up in the trees for long, smooth single vines that can be easily pulled down. (If the vines are funny-looking, however, avoid them—they could be poison ivy.) If you are not so ambitious, a wide variety of natural and dried vines are available at any craft or flower store.

The first step is to separate and group the vines according to their length and width. This will help ensure an even flow from one vine to the next when winding the basket.

1 Start with a good, sturdy vine and bend it into a circle, passing the vine over and under itself to lock in the handle. Then shift directions and create another circular form, laying it perpendicular to the original. These two circles will form the base and the handle of the finished basket, thus determining the basket's final dimensions. The larger the circle, the wider or deeper the basket and the higher the handle.

2 The fun starts when you take the wisteria, or any other manageable vine, and weave the body of the basket. Start in the middle of the perpendicular circles and weave the first vine over and under, over and under, in a circular motion around the base. How tightly you wrap the vine will determine how dense the finished basket will be.

© Ralph Bogertman

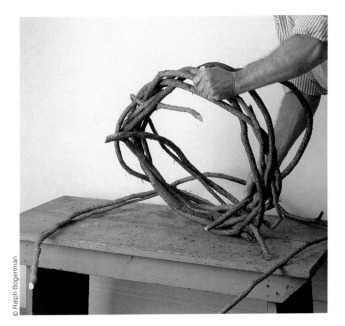

© Ralph Bogertman

$\mathcal{A}$bove: *Here the vine is woven into the body of the basket. Weave it over and under in a circular motion around the base.*

3 Gradually draw the outer vine wraps in tighter to form a basket shape. As you establish the proportions, pass the vine over and under itself to lock it into the desired shape.

4 When you have the basic form completed, go back and fill in the basket with thinner vines until you achieve the desired shape and density. What you are doing is filling in space with the vine. If you want to fill out a particular area, simply add more vines to fill in the blanks.

5 After the form is completed, secure the ends by either tucking them in for a neater, more unified look, or leaving them dangling for a wild, unkempt look.

To create a handle for the basket, bring a long vine up from the bottom, turn it downward and then back through the bottom (above, left and right). As with the body, the more vines you use and the tighter you pull them, the more dense the handle will be (left). You may decide that you want to use a single vine for the handle, or more, for a fuller, thicker look.

© Ralph Bogertman

TWIG PLANT STAND

Materials needed:

Four 30-inch-long (76-centimeters-long) twigs
Four 16-inch-long (41-centimeters-long) twigs
Sixteen 20-inch-long (51-centimeters-long) twigs
Twenty 12-inch-long (31-centimeters-long) twigs
1½ inch (4-centimeter) flat-head nails

Note: Try to find twigs of a uniform diameter (about an inch [3 centimeters]), except for the four 30-inch twigs, which should be about 1¼ inches (3 centimeters) in diameter.

1 To begin the planter, lay two 20-inch (51-centimeter) twigs on your worktable. They should be 8 inches (20 centimeters) apart and parallel. Keeping a 1-inch (2.5-centimeter) overlap, place a 12-inch (31-centimeter) twig on each end and nail in place.

2 Repeat this process, alternating between sets of 20-inch (51-centimeter) and 12-inch (31-centimeter) twigs until the planter box reaches the desired height. (The planter box illustrated is 6½ inches [17 centimeters] tall.)

3 To add legs, place one of the 30-inch (76-centimeter) twigs on the inside corner of the planter box and nail in place. Repeat for each corner.

4 To anchor the legs, add a cross piece 5½ inches (14 centimeters) off the floor. Nail in place. Secure the back of the planter to front with two 20-inch (51-centimeter) twigs. To brace the side of the planter stand, nail on four 16-inch (41-centimeter) twigs, two on top and two under the horizontal twig.

5 Add the V brace with two 20-inch (51-centimeter) twigs. Nail to secure in place.

TWIG TABLE

Materials needed:

*Forty-four 20-inch (51-centimeter) twigs as close to the
  same diameter as possible*

1½-inch (4-centimeter) flat-head nails

hammer

1 Begin by selecting two twigs of uniform dimension for the bottom. They should be as flat as possible; you may want to sand the bottoms to ensure stability.

2 Allowing a 1-inch (2.5-centimeter) overlap, place two more twigs on top of and perpendicular to the base twigs. Secure with a nail.

3 Repeat this process of placing two twigs on top of the preceding twigs, log-cabin style, until you have reached the desired height.

4 To make a top for the table, lay twigs across the top, no more than ¼ inch (.6 centimeters) apart.

5 You may use the table as it stands, or finish it with a piece of ¼-inch- (.6-centimeters) thick glass. (Make sure the glass has polished edges for safety.)

© Ralph Bogertman

FURTHER READING

Duncan, Thomas. **How to Buy and Restore Wicker Furniture.** Syracuse, Indiana: Duncan-Holmes Publishing Co., 1983.

Heywood Brothers and Wakefield Co. Classic Wicker Furniture: Complete 1898-1899 Illustrated Catalog. Mineola, NY: Dover Publications, 1982.

Miller, Bruce and Widess, Jim. **The Caner's Handbook.** New York: Prentice Hall, 1983

Osborn, Susan. **American Rustic Furniture.** New York: Harmony Books, 1984.

Saunders, Richard. **Collecting and Restoring Wicker Furniture.** New York: Crown Publishers, 1976.

Wilk, Christopher. **Thonet: 150 Years of Furniture.** Woodbury, NY: Barron's, 1980.

SOURCES

The following listings represent manufacturers, importers, dealers, suppliers, and craftspeople associated with wicker, cane, and/or willow. Most sell directly to the public; the few that sell to designers only are indicated with an asterisk.

Amish Country Collection
R.D. 5, Sunset Valley Road
New Castle, PA 16105

Backwoods Furnishings
Box 161, Rte. 28
Indian Lake, NY 12842

The Basket Artist
P.O. Box 438
Baraboo, WI 53193

*Bielecky Brothers, Inc.
306 East 61st Street
New York, NY 10021

Cane and Basket Supply Co.
1283 South Cochran Avenue
Los Angeles, CA 90019

The Caning Shop
926 Gilman Street
Berkeley, CA 94710

Clark Casual Furniture, Inc.
214 Industrial Road
P.O. Box N
Greensburg, KY 42743

Comanche Design
3019 1/2 Olympic Boulevard
Santa Monica, CA 90404

Connecticut Cane & Reed Co.
P.O. Box 762
134 Pine Street
Manchester, CT 06040

*Conrad Imports, Inc.
575 Tenth Street
San Francisco, CA 94103

Copper Kettle Antiques
160 Monmouth Street
Red Bank, NJ 07701

Country Manor
P.O. Box 520, Dept. WCW
Sperryville, VA 22740

D & F Wicker Imports
1050 Route 46
Box 479
Ledgewood, NJ 07852

Mary K. Darrah Twig and Rustic Furniture
33 Ferry Street
New Hope, PA 18938

Deutsch
31 East 32 Street
New York, NY 10016

European Furniture Industries Inc.
4900-A Bakers Ferry Road
Atlanta, GA 30336

Ficks Reed
4900 Charlemar Drive
Cincinnati, OH 45227

Frank's Cane and Rush Supply
7252 Heil Avenue
Huntington Beach, CA 92647

The Gazebo of New York
660 Madison Avenue
New York, NY 10021

The Gazebo of New York
The Galleria II
5085 Westheimer, Suite 2585
Houston, TX 77056

The Gazebo of New York
South Coast Plaza
3333 Bristol Street
Costa Mesa, CA 92626

GMS Imports, Inc.
11400 N.W. 65th Place
Fort Lauderdale, FL 33309

Grand Rattan Furniture Company
53-06 Grand Avenue
Maspeth, NY 11378

*International Contract Furnishings
305 East 63 Street
New York, NY 10021

Ikea Inc.
Plymouth Commons
Plymouth Meeting, PA 19462

Kelter-Malce Antiques
361 Bleecker Street
New York, NY 10014

*Knoll International
655 Madison Avenue
New York, NY 10021

Lodgepole Furniture
Star Rte., Box 15
Jackson, WY 83001